The Greatest Guide to

Your Dream Wedding

This is a **GREATEST**GUIDES title

Greatest Guides Limited, Woodstock, Bridge End, Warwick CV34 6PD, United Kingdom

www.greatestguides.com

Series created by Harshad Kotecha

Greatest Guides is committed to a sustainable future for our planet. This book is printed on paper certified by the Forest Stewardship Council.

MIX
Paper
FSC   FSC® C020837

Printed and bound in the United Kingdom

ISBN 978-1-907906-06-0

To Colin with all my love.

Without you,
none of this would have been possible.

Contents

Acknowledgements

My thanks for help and advice go to:

Jennifer Baker Photography

Harewood Cars

Belair Video

Prudence Gowns

Marldon Marquees

Celebration Balloons

Amanda Dow, Beauty Therapist

Kelly Williams at Toni and Guy

Su Kopil, Una Westney, Janine White (USA)

Sandra Beswetherick, Kathy Burrough, Elizabeth von Aderkas (Canada)

Claire Bennett (Australia)

A few words from Jill …

So you've done it! You've found the man of your dreams
and have named the day. Note here that I'm addressing the
bride. More on the bridegroom later, but, be assured that,
unless the man you've managed to get to propose to you is
a real 'New Man', the rest of the wedding will fall on your
shoulders. He might tag along to wedding fairs and make
suitable noises in the background, but the decisions will
undoubtedly be all yours. The best you can hope for is that
he will turn up, suitably dressed, on the day.

There are two things you've got to be prepared for when
planning a wedding. The first is the cost. Forget the amount
you first thought of – the final cost will be at least four times
that. But hopefully this book will help you save money while
still having the wedding of your dreams.

The second thing is that there will be rows and arguments.
Big, fiery fights, or small smoldering resentments, there
has probably never yet been a wedding without them. You
might smile and say it couldn't happen to you – but don't
believe it. It could be the choice of venue, the bridesmaids,
or the guest list, but arguments there will be! After 10 years
of running a wedding business, I've seen it all!

So this book is intended to guide you through the minefield
of planning your wedding, so that you can walk down the
aisle on your big day, confident that everything will go well
because everything that could possibly go wrong has been
neatly avoided.

Certificate of Marriage

This Certifies that _____ and _____ were united in marriage on this day _____ and _____

This ceremony was witnessed and cel_____ and _____

Legally Binding

“ Happiness is being married to your best friend. **”**

Anon

Chapter 1
Legally Binding

You're engaged! You've named the day!

Wherever you live in the world, when you decide that you want to get married, weddings are special occasions. Although there are bound to be differences in traditions and customs throughout the world, even within different areas of individual countries, everyone wants their wedding to be the same – a happy, joyous occasion that flows without anything going wrong. This book aims to take you through all the preparations for your special day, so that you can enjoy it without stress.

It is based on mainstream church and civil ceremonies within the legal systems of the USA, UK, Canada and Australia, but couples from any country and members of other faiths will also find it invaluable.

I haven't given prices and fees as they vary so much throughout the world and change from year to year. However, there are plenty of money-saving ideas for everyone, so you can keep within your budget.

In addition, I have included some of the traditions and superstitions connected with weddings.

The law

Before you start planning your wedding, you need to know if you are legally able to marry and what types of wedding are available to you, so let's get the formalities out of the way first.

USA

Marriage laws vary from state to state within the USA, so it is vital that you check the requirements with your local marriage license office or county clerk. However, every couple will need to obtain a license before the marriage can take place. To obtain the license, you may need to apply in person, and you will need to provide proof of identity. The license is only valid for a certain length of time; again, this varies from state to state.

Many states require proof that you are medically fit to marry, and that you are free from certain diseases, although most no longer specify an actual medical test.

You can have a religious ceremony carried out by an official of that religion, such as a priest, minister or rabbi. Civil weddings are carried out by judges or JP's.

UK

All weddings in England, Wales and Northern Ireland must take place in an Anglican church, or any other religious building registered for the solemnization of marriage, a Register Office, or a building approved for civil marriage.

If you want to get married in a Church of England or Church in Wales, you should speak to the vicar of the parish. You would not also normally need to see the Registrar of your district.

For other religious buildings, you need to speak to the person in charge of marriages first of all. You will need to give notice at the Register Office(s) of the district(s) in which you live. Some faiths will also require you to book the services of a Registrar in order to register the marriage (see how to do this in the Civil Weddings section).

Scotland has different laws to England and Wales and details are given in the Church and Civil Weddings chapters.

Canada

You will need to obtain a marriage license from your local municipal clerk's office a few weeks before your wedding. For this, you will need proof of both your identity and your age.

Marriages can also be solemnized under the authority of banns in a church, where both parties worship at that church. You must speak to the minister about this before booking any dates.

Weddings in Canada are carried out by either a minister or member of the clergy registered under the Marriage Act, or by a judge or JP.

Australia

The person who conducts a wedding in Australia is known as the Celebrant. Bride and groom plus their celebrant must sign and lodge a Notice of Intended Marriage from one month and one day before the wedding date. Proof of ID will be required. They also need to make a statutory declaration that they know of no impediment to the marriage. You can have a religious or civil ceremony.

Second time around – wherever you live

If you have been married before, you will need to produce evidence that you are free to remarry. This will either be a divorce certificate (Decree Absolute in the UK) in the case of a divorced person or a Death Certificate if the person has been widowed.

If either of you have been divorced and you wish to be married in church, you need to speak to the minister first. Many faiths will not allow divorced people to remarry in church, although they may well offer a blessing ceremony. However, some of the non-conformist churches will allow remarriage after divorce.

The rest of the book applies to everyone – with a few minor differences – wherever you happen to live.

Now You've Named the Day

" Love does not consist of gazing at each other but in looking forward in the same direction. "

Antoine de Saint-Exupéry

Chapter 2
Now You've Named the Day

Now we've got the boring formalities out of the way, the fun starts.

Be prepared!

When planning a wedding, the golden rule to remember is that, at some time, you will offend someone. It might be your parents, your future in-laws or the parents of hopeful bridesmaids. Don't worry; stay calm and the argument will blow over. Just remember that it is YOUR wedding and, while you want to try and keep everyone happy, it's not always possible. You are not alone. It happens to ALL couples!

What if… ?

What happens if the reception venue is double- booked? What happens if your wedding dress shop goes bankrupt? No, you don't want to think of things like that happening to you, but they can. The bigger the wedding, the more things there are to go wrong, so wedding insurance is a MUST. A specialist wedding insurance package can cost as little as a romantic dinner for two, but, when you think that the average wedding these days runs into thousands, it's a minor expense that can be worth every penny if things go wrong.

You can get details of wedding insurance packages from any of the big insurance companies but also check out leaflets at wedding fairs. Many smaller specialist companies, and even supermarkets, also offer very good deals.

Ideas!

Have an idea about the type of wedding you want before you start booking anything. If you want the traditional church white wedding, then you will need to look for suitable venues. However, you might want to be different and have some sort of themed wedding, e.g. Medieval or Roaring Twenties. In that case, it is no use booking somewhere totally out of keeping with the theme. Changing your mind after booking a venue can be very costly, as you would almost certainly lose your deposit.

Research

In these hi-tech days, it's easy to find all your wedding requirements on the internet and this can save loads of time. However, seeing places or things on a screen can be misleading. Reception rooms, for example, can look huge in photographs, but, in reality, can be very cramped. Unless you live far from the area you've chosen to get married in, it's important that you view everything in person. That way you won't be disappointed on the day.

Wedding fairs are held all over the country, both in actual wedding venues and large exhibition halls. Those at hotels, etc. are likely to involve local companies and will give you an idea of what is available in your chosen area. The large fairs will have hundreds of stands and thousands of ideas, often with huge prices. Leave your credit card at home but take a notebook and jot down those that appeal to you. Keep a folder with brochures and cards in. You won't use most of them, but they're great fun to look at – and you might just find the perfect theme for your day.

Make a list

Make a list of all the jobs to be done and tick them off as you go. It's a good idea to make a wedding calendar – you can use a cheap diary – to show when final meetings have to take place and when deposits and final payments have to be made. You don't want to find that your cars have been canceled because you forgot to pay the balance on time.

Help or hindrance?

You might want to accept any offers of help going, especially if it eases your financial burden. But, sometimes, things can get a bit fraught and, having seen her handiwork, you might not want Aunty Olive to make your bouquet/dress/cake. Time to be tactful. A good way out is to invent a mythical friend and say, gently, "I'm so sorry. Mary at work offered and I've already told her I'm using Flowers'r'Us. She'd be so offended if she found out you were doing them, I might even lose my job…"

Paying the bills

Many couples find it useful to set up a separate wedding account with their bank. This means that they can put in regular amounts of money to be used solely for the wedding, without having to dip into their everyday budget.

Who pays what?

Traditionally, the bride's parents footed the bill for the whole day but these days, luckily for them, things are far more flexible. Some couples choose to pay for everything themselves; others share with both sets of parents. If this is going to be the case, it is diplomatic to set up a meeting with the family and discuss who is going to pay for what. It's not a good idea to simply tell one set of parents that they are expected to dig deep!

The guest list

Who to ask? This is always big problem and will be where you'll wish the two of you had just eloped! Your budget will have a big bearing on this – see the Reception section for calculations – but once you have your number, it's time to sit down and work out your list. The obvious people are your immediate families, plus your attendants and best man.

It is diplomatic to try and get an even number on both sides, but sizes of families and circle of friends vary, so this is not always possible.

Children

To invite children or not? If you have your own children, you can't really <u>not</u> invite others. If you have a big family with lots of children, it will probably be accepted that they are all going to be present. This can add to the costs considerably. You will need to ask if there is a reduction in price for children's meals at your reception venue.

Many couples feel that children will prove to be a distraction at their wedding. If you choose not to invite them, remember that you might well cause offence to those parents who feel that they should be there. Another consideration is that some guests might not be able to attend if they have no-one with whom to leave their children.

If you decide on a 'no children' rule, you will also have to decide what age you define as children. You might not want toddlers running around when speeches are being made, but 13-year-olds are a different kettle of fish!

Too many?

If you find that you have more people you want to invite than your budget will allow, you will have to be very strict about those you ask to the wedding itself. Others further out from the main set of family or friends will be more than happy to simply be invited to the evening do, if you are choosing to have one.

Animals!

For some couples, the day would not be complete without their pets being present, especially dogs. Always check with the venue to see if animals are allowed. If they are, ask someone reliable to look after them on the day. You don't want to have to go walkies in your wedding finery!

Stationery

Once you have decided on your guest list, you will need to actually invite people. Traditionally, invitations were sent out only six weeks before the wedding day, but, these days, they tend to be sent much earlier, especially if guests live a distance away and will have to make travel or hotel arrangements.

Where?

You can have wedding stationery printed by specialist suppliers. All will have huge catalogs of samples for you to choose from, ranging from traditional formal through to pretty floral and quirky modern designs.

Many high street stores and supermarkets sell blanks for you to complete yourselves. This can be a cheaper option, but you might not be able to get a full selection of cards, such as Order of Service.

Card-making is a popular hobby at the moment, although this is not necessarily a cheaper option. However, you will have the satisfaction of knowing that your stationery is personal to you. You can always go and look at a sample book in a specialist shop to get ideas of the wording to use!

What?

The most important item you will require is a set of invitations. Don't be tempted to order one per person. You just need one per family, unless you are inviting adult children from the same house, in which case, it is polite to send them a separate invitation.

You might want to choose a design that includes a reply card so that your guests have no excuse for not replying. You will need to give final numbers to your reception venue several weeks beforehand, so make sure you give a date by which recipients must reply.

If you are having an evening function, you will also need invitations to this. They will have different wording and will make it clear that the recipient is only invited to that function, not to the wedding itself.

For a church wedding, you might want to have Orders of Service with the words of hymns, etc. printed. If you are saving money, these are not absolutely necessary as a church will provide hymn books. Many people, though, especially the older relatives, like to keep an Order of Service as a souvenir of the wedding.

Place cards are very important, especially if you are having a sit-down meal for your reception. Again, these can be ordered to match your set of stationery, but you can also use plain white cards available from any stationery shop. Try to get someone who is good at calligraphy to write the names on the cards.

Menus can also be useful (see the Reception section).

Don't forget that you will need to send thank you letters after the wedding. Again, you can buy a set to match the rest of your stationery but you might want to produce your own (see the Happy Ever After section).

Nothing like the present

These days most people expect a couple to provide a present list. This can take the form of your own printed list, or details of a store where you have set up a list. Most of the big stores will provide this service and you need to contact the one(s) you wish to deal with, as they will each have their own method. Most, these days, will set up an online list so that your guests can either buy instore or via the internet.

It's a good idea to ask around and find out other people's opinions of the service provided. Some stores are better than others at getting the right presents to couples on time.

Wedding showers

These are usual in many countries but not in the UK. They are for females only and organized by the Maid of Honor (see the Dancing Attendance chapter) and possibly by another female relative or work colleague as well.

Present or money?

Many couples, these days, feel that they have everything they need. You might have your own flat, been living together, or it could be your second time around.

So you might think that you'd like money – possibly to go towards a large item, such as a dishwasher. If so, you need to say this (tactfully) with your invitation. However, some people dislike giving money so it's a good idea to also provide a list of items. Don't be afraid to think laterally when drawing up a list. You might not need another toaster, but if you're moving from a flat to a house, what about garden tools? A camera? Or items for a joint interest? You never know, you might just get that surfboard you've always wanted!

If you definitely only want money, be aware that some people (especially the older generation) can be ill at ease, or embarrassed, by not knowing how much to give. A way round this is to tell everyone that you will have a bucket or – much prettier – a wishing well for donations of checks (cheques) or cash. By doing this, guests can simply put in cash without disclosing the amount. You could attach a notebook so donors could sign their names.

Your thank you letters (see the Happy Ever After section) would then simply thank the donor for their generous gift and for sharing your day.

A current trend is to request donations towards a luxury honeymoon – often arranged via an online specialist travel company. Most younger guests will be happy to do this, but, again, as above, some older relatives might not know how much to give. Others dislike the impersonal nature of a credit card over the phone, or an email confirmation. Some, too, will mutter that you should pay for your own honeymoon!

Church Weddings

" To have and to hold,
from this day forward;
for better, for worse,
for richer, for poorer,
in sickness and in health,
to love and to cherish,
till death us do part; **"**

Book of Common Prayer – Marriage Service

Chapter 3
Church Weddings

Different faiths in each country have different rules on who can get married in their churches, so you must make an appointment to meet with the religious leader of that faith to discuss their requirements.

USA

Religious ceremonies must be conducted under the customs of the particular religion by an official of that faith, such as a priest, minister or rabbi.

If you want a religious wedding ceremony out of doors, check very carefully before planning it. Most dioceses of the Roman Catholic Church have a regulation that requires that the bishop's permission is needed for a wedding outside a church building.

Similarly, ministers of the Episcopalian Church will perform a wedding ceremony outside but, if you are taking the Eucharist, the ceremony must be carried out inside a church building. Episcopalian ceremonies must use the marriage service from the Book of Common Prayer.

UK

In England and Wales, you must first check that your chosen church is registered for "the solemnization of marriage". Most Anglican churches are, but there are some non-conformist churches that are not. It does not mean that you cannot get married in them, simply that you will also need a

Registrar present. A Roman Catholic Church will require a license from the Registrar of your district.

Anglican Church

Before you can get married, you must have the Banns read in the parishes where you both live (and in the parish in which you are getting married, if this is somewhere different). The Banns are an announcement of your intention to wed and they give people the opportunity to object if they so wish. They have to be read for three Sundays in the three months before your wedding date. These are usually consecutive but do not have to be.

Instead of Banns, you can apply for a common license but you will need to discuss this with the minister.

If you want a religious ceremony in Scotland, it can take place anywhere you choose, providing the minister is happy with your choice of venue. This means that you could have an outdoor wedding (weather and midges permitting!). Unlike in England, the banns are not published, though you will have to apply for a license no later than 15 days before the wedding.

Canada and Australia

The rules are very similar to the UK, but Banns are not necessarily read.

Wherever you live, you will need to make an appointment to meet with your minister or priest.

First meeting

Many churches will ask you to attend marriage preparation sessions. Some may ask you to attend services on a regular basis. The vicar might well discuss the form of service you want to use, e.g. the traditional or modern service.

The minister will also discuss the fees you will need to pay. The standard fee will cover the publication of the banns, the marriage service and the certificate of marriage. There might well be other expenses, such as the choir, bells, etc.

In a queue

Ask how many other weddings might be taking place on your chosen date. Popular churches get very busy, especially in the summer season, and can have up to five or six weddings on the same day, allowing only one and a quarter hours for each. This is usually adequate, but you will need to tell your photographer so that he/she can make allowances and possibly arrange a second venue for photos.

If music be the food of love

Hymns are a very important part of the church service and most vicars will have a list of the most popular choices. However, you might want to choose some that are special to you. This is great, and will make the service more personal to you, providing the rest of the congregation know them, too. Imagine a large church with the organ playing and only one or two people trying to sing along with an unknown hymn. Sometimes traditional ways are best!

Grand entrance

If you decide against the traditional wedding marches to walk down the aisle, make sure the organist knows the music you want played. Don't end up like the couple who requested the very romantic love song from "Robin Hood, Prince of Thieves" (*Everything I Do* by Bryan Adams) but actually left the church to "Robin Hood, Robin Hood, Riding through the Glen".

Choir

Most churches have a choir and there will be a charge for it to sing at your wedding. This might be a set fee, or a fee per choir member. If this is the case, ask how many choir members are expected to attend, so that you know how much you are likely to pay.

Recording the moment

When you first meet your minister, one of the questions you need to ask is about photography. Some churches will not allow photography, while the ceremony is taking place. If this is the case, you will need to make this clear to your photographer/video recordist.

Flowers

A church always looks beautiful when it is decorated with flowers for your wedding. If there are any other weddings taking place on the same day as yours, it might be possible to share the cost of the flowers with the other couple(s).

Although your florist will supply arrangements for the church, you might find that the person who normally arranges the flowers for regular church services is willing to do them. They are often very skilled and will know what sizes and shapes suit each part of the church. This usually works out a lot cheaper as well.

You might be limited to the color and choice of flowers at certain times of the religious calendar. Again, check this well before the actual day.

Practice make perfect

Most churches will offer you the chance to have a rehearsal a couple of days before the wedding day. Take advantage of this, so that everyone knows what they have to do on the day. Usually, the rehearsal will be for the couple, their parents, bridesmaids and best man. If the ushers have never been to the particular church before, it is a good idea if they go, too, so that they can see where everyone will be seated.

Shhhhh

A church wedding service is meant to be a serious occasion and can sometimes be spoiled by children shouting out or running around. So, if you or your guests have children who will be present at the service, it is a good idea to take them to church a couple of times before the wedding day so that they get used to the building and the sense of occasion. Large churches can be frightening to small children who have never been in one before. Also, they might not be used to sitting quietly for any length of time, an explanation of the service and the people involved would be helpful.

Fashionably late

Tradition says that the bride arrives a few minutes late. This is usually acceptable, but if there are several weddings on the same day, even five minutes delay can put all the following weddings out. You don't want to be having your photos taken while the next bride is drawing up in her car.

Order of Service

After you have had photos taken as you arrive at the church, the vicar will almost certainly meet the bride and whoever is giving her away at the church door and escort them to the front of the church. If you are having a choir, they may well form a procession in front of you.

The service itself will have been explained to you at either the preparation sessions or the rehearsal.

Signing the Register

After the service, the bride and groom plus witnesses will need to sign the register. This is sometimes done in view of the congregation but is often done in the vestry. To avoid confusion, you will need to decide beforehand who is to go with you to sign; it is usually both sets of parents but need not be.

Procession

Once the service is over, the bride and groom will lead the guests out of church. It is customary for the bride's father to escort the groom's mother and vice versa. The best man will escort the chief bridesmaid. If there are equal numbers of bridesmaids and groomsmen, they will follow on in order.

If either of the mothers do not have a partner, it is courteous to ask a close male relative or friend to stand in, so that she doesn't have to walk on her own.

Call of nature

Remember that most churches don't have toilets. Always research where the highest gravestone is, because, without exception, a child will want to GO during the service. Likewise, it's not unknown for the groom or best man to need the toilet, either because of nerves or from too many 'confidence boosters' at the nearest pub beforehand. However, kind clergymen are used to this and will usually find somewhere for them.

Confetti

A shower of confetti makes a wonderful photo as you leave the wedding venue. However, check that the venue will allow it. Many churches have banned the use, as it is so difficult to clear up afterwards. It is now possible to get bio-degradable confetti, which might be allowed – but you would have to make this clear to your guests before the wedding!

Other options include rice and flower petals.

Rice is usually gathered up by birds and small animals after the wedding but can be very sharp if thrown straight at you. It can also be dangerous if thrown near eyes.

Dried flower petals are very pretty, especially if you provide them to match your color scheme. Florists will often provide them as part of your package, along with little cones to hand out to your guests. If you choose to do this, someone will have to be responsible for handing them out to guests.

A cheaper option is to buy bags of petals and make the cones yourself, from colored paper or old sheets of music. Again, someone will have to be responsible for taking care of them and handing them out to guests. Make sure it's someone reliable who won't wander off and leave them!

The bells, the bells!

The sound of the bells ringing is linked with weddings. Like the choir, the cost of the bell ringers will not be included in the basic price of the service. If the church has a peal of bells, they will usually ring out as the bride arrives, then as the couple leave the church, and for some time afterwards.

Bells can be very loud. If you are having a video made of the day, check with your video company that the noise of the bells can be faded, or it will overpower the rest of the sounds and conversation.

A little snack!

There is often quite a long time between the start of a wedding and sitting down to eat at the reception. This is especially so if guests have had to travel some distance even before the ceremony starts. Children can become very bad-tempered and disruptive if they are hungry, so you could provide a few boxes of biscuits or packets of crisps and cartons of drinks with straws to keep them going. They can be produced from a car's boot by a willing helper. You'll probably find that it won't only be children who take advantage, especially if there are some cool drinks on a hot day. It won't cost very much and can make a lot of difference to frayed tempers!

Civil Weddings

" When you meet someone who can cook and do housework – don't hesitate a minute – marry him! **"**

Anon

Chapter 4
Civil Weddings

USA

Civil weddings in the USA are conducted by a judge or a person licensed to conduct weddings. Contrary to popular belief, this does not include a ship's captain!

Laws vary between states, so it is vital that you check the legal requirements before planning your wedding. You will always need to apply for a marriage license. These have an expiry date so make sure you've applied for one that is valid for the date of your wedding. You will need to provide proof that you are legally allowed to marry.

In some states, you can marry as soon as you have the license, but others make you wait for a few days.

Although civil weddings can take place in a court-house or town hall, this practice seems to be declining, with couples choosing other, more attractive venues.

UK

Unlike much of the rest of the world, there are very strict rules in the UK as to where you can get married.

A civil wedding is one that is held in a Register Office (Registration Office in Scotland) or an approved venue. Marriages cannot be held out of doors in England and Wales but can be in Scotland, providing the venue is an approved one. You can find a list of approved venues in your area from your local Register Office or on www.gro.gov.uk.

Register Office weddings are still a very popular choice in the UK, so information on them is given here in detail.

Many Register Offices now operate an appointments system so always ring first, rather than just turning up to try and book your wedding.

For either a wedding in the Register Office or at an approved venue, you need to give 'Notice of Marriage' at least 15 days before your chosen date, with required evidence. Both of you need to attend the Register Office. You need to have resided in the area for at least 7 days prior to giving notice. Your Notice of Marriage will be displayed on a notice board in the Register Office, for anyone to view.

Registering for a marriage

You will need to give the Superintendent Registrar:

Your name.
Proof of age.
Proof of residency, e.g. passport.

If you have been married before, you will also need:

Divorce Decree Absolute, or
Death Certificate of your former spouse.

You will not be able to take out an actual Notice of Marriage more than one year before your wedding, although you may be able to book an approved venue and a Registrar's services longer in advance. Your venue will be able to advise you on the procedure for that. Popular venues get booked very early, so it is a good idea to get your venue booked, even if you can't confirm the time until you've been in touch with the Registrar.

Register Office

These vary. Some are in beautiful buildings, others in council offices. However, nowadays, ceremonies in these offices have lost their hole-in-acorner, rushed-wedding reputation and are generally dignified occasions, with many personal touches. Most now offer a range of ceremonies, the cheapest of which being a basic ceremony in the presence of two witnesses. Others offer longer (and more expensive) personalized ceremonies.

Good timing

Register Offices can be very busy places, especially on a Saturday. One late wedding will hold up everyone else's, so make sure that you and your guests are on time. This is not a place for the bride to be traditionally late. The Registrar can cancel your wedding if you are not there at the proper time.

Parking is sometimes limited at Register Offices so advise your guests to leave extra time if they need to park elsewhere. If they have never visited the town before, it is a good idea to provide a map of the area, with the nearest car parks marked – and an idea of the cost so that they can have the right change ready.

Canada and Australia

Like the USA, weddings in town halls are declining in number, with couples choosing their own venues. You can get married out of doors in both countries, although there may be a fee to the local council if you use a municipal park.

Wherever you live

Size matters

If you decide to get married in a Register Office or a hotel, always check how many guests can be accommodated. It is no good booking a room that will only hold 30 people if you know you want at least 100 guests. Most hotel ceremony rooms and Register Offices are far smaller than churches.

Some venues will limit the number of bridesmaids they will allow because of the space available at the front of the wedding room. This might be worth checking if you want to have several attendants.

Personal touch

Although you might be able to choose the vows, words, and music at your ceremony, you should be aware that they must be non-religious. Also, they must not be edited to leave out any religious references. Many Registrars/celebrants will have a book with a choice of suggested words and readings. However, if you have a special piece you would like to use, you should make sure that it is approved at least seven days before the ceremony. You should give both the names of the author and the person who is going to read the piece. This gives time for it to be included in the ceremony (also see the Getting Personal chapter).

The law does not require you to exchange rings, but most couples do, so you will need to discuss the promises that will be made at that point in the ceremony.

Choosing a venue

Civil wedding venues can range from stately homes to sports stadiums, and facilities will vary from place to place. Always go and view the ones that you like the look of and speak to the wedding co-ordinator. Many will arrange wedding fairs throughout the year. This gives you a good chance to see the facilities set up for a wedding.

Most, but not all, will offer a marriage ceremony and reception package. Some only offer the room for the ceremony and you will have to find another venue for your reception.

Not a cheap option

Don't automatically assume that a civil wedding is a cheaper option than a church one. If you decide to get married in a hotel, you will probably be quoted an all-inclusive price. This might seem like a good deal but almost certainly doesn't include the celebrant's fee. You will have to pay for him to attend the ceremony and this will be far higher than the fee you would pay at the actual Register Office or town hall, and can add to your overall budget.

Co-ordination

Most approved venues will have a wedding co-ordinator (see Receptions).

Always ask what is provided in the ceremony room, and how it will be arranged. Don't assume that there will be flowers. You might have to provide these yourself.

Some venues will have a selection of music that will be played while guests are waiting, and for you to enter and leave the room to. If you have favorite music, you will need to provide this in advance and make sure that any CD is clearly labeled with the number of the track you have chosen.

If you are going to have live music during your ceremony, tell your venue, as equipment might need to be set up in advance. Your guests don't want to be tripping over trailing flexes and the last thing you need in your commitment ceremony is the sound of instruments tuning up or the feedback from the amps.

In the open air

Most countries (but not England and Wales) will allow civil weddings to take place out of doors. If you live somewhere where the weather is almost guaranteed, then this can be a really romantic occasion.

Wineries, hotel gardens or your own pretty backyard can make ideal wedding settings. If you choose to go to a hotel or recognized wedding venue, the staff will make sure that all is put in place for you. However, if you want to use your own garden, look at the facilities that you'll need.

In your garden

The Getting a Good Reception chapter gives details of marquee hire, chairs and the all-important toilets.

If you want to play music at the wedding, check out the music system beforehand. Speakers that sound very loud indoors might not have the same impact outside. You may need to borrow or hire a professional sound system. That applies to making your vows as well. Even a light breeze can whisk your words away, so that none of your guests can hear your promises.

Parking needs to be considered. If you have a large drive that will accommodate all the expected cars, then there's no problem. However, if extra space is needed, check out the local area and tell guests the best place to leave their cars. They don't want to be driving round looking for a place to park while panicking about missing the ceremony.

Leaving it all behind

You might decide that you want to leave everything behind and escape to somewhere exotic to get married. A destination wedding can be a wonderful idea and surely the most romantic wedding photos are those taken on a golden beach with a deep blue sea behind you?

Making it legal

Vows taken on a moonlit beach when you're on holiday might be romantic but are unlikely to be legal. It is important that you know what the law is.

If you want to get married somewhere different, you can make all the arrangements yourself, using the internet to check out the laws for individual countries or states.

However, many tour operators and wedding companies now offer wedding packages. This means that they will make sure the marriage will be legal in your own country or state. Most well-known names are reliable companies, but things can still go wrong. It is just as important, if not more so, to take out wedding insurance.

Always double check the documents you need to take with you.

Check first

Before you make your booking, ask the travel company if they can put you in touch with couples who have got married at the same resort, or look on some of the websites dedicated to giving unbiased views of hotels and resorts.

Weather

Research the average weather conditions at your chosen time of year. You don't want to spend all your money on a luxury wedding in the Caribbean, only to find that it is hurricane season and that your wedding could be canceled due to the storms.

Who to take?

If you want the wedding to be just for the two of you, that's fine. However, many couples decide to make the occasion a family holiday and take parents, children and attendants with them. If this is what you want to do, always discuss it with the family first. Make sure who is paying for what and check that everyone can afford to go.

Think about the family and decide if they are going to be able to get along with each other for a whole holiday. People who can get on with each other for a day at home might not manage two weeks together. You don't want your wedding spoiled by squabbling relatives.

Dressing-up

Clothes for weddings abroad in covered in the Dressed to Impress section.

And after?

Many couples choose to have a reception or party after they return, so that the family and friends who were not able to attend the wedding can celebrate. This can be quite an informal affair and can be arranged like the evening occasions in the Reception section. Apart from seeing all your family and friends, it's a good opportunity to wear the wedding dress again!

Getting Personal

❝ Marriage – the beautiful blending of two lives, two hearts, two loves. ❞

Anon

Chapter 5
Getting Personal

Do you want your wedding to be different to all the others you've been to? If so, you can personalize your ceremony in all sorts of ways.

What could be more romantic than making your own vows to each other at your wedding? And what about a personal choice of music or a special reading or piece of poetry?

Vows

Some churches insist on vows from their religious book, and, in most countries, there are statutory declarations that have to be made at a civil wedding. However, there are rarely any objections to you adding promises of your own.

Writing your own vows needs preparation. It's no good thinking you can just scribble some off the night before the wedding. In any case, you'll need to discuss their use with your marriage celebrant when arrangements are being made. You also need to make sure that both of you are happy to speak the vows before your guests, without getting embarrassed.

Your vows needn't be long and involved, but they do need to be sincere. They are also intended to be witnessed by your guests, not just a private conversation between the pair of you.

Allow yourselves several sessions of "quiet" time where just the two of you can let your thoughts flow. Arm yourselves with plenty of paper, so that you can jot down ideas, however stilted or silly they may seem at first.

Ask yourselves:

- What do you love about each other?
- What are your hopes for the future?
- What are your fears?
- What do you want to promise each other?

Now think about what style you want. Are they going to be traditional words, flowery, funny? Yes – you can be funny and still be sincere.

Here are some ideas to get you thinking:

A statement of your love – to put before or after the statutory declarations

Many people spend their lives searching for their one true love. Some people are lucky to find the person they can truly call their soulmate, while others spend the rest of their lives searching and never finding. I am happy to count myself among the lucky ones, because I certainly found you.

Modern and romantic

Her: *I Xxxxxx take you Xxxxxx to be my lifelong husband. Since the day we met, I have loved everything about you – your strength, your patience and your wonderful sense of humor. I promise not to try and change you but to accept that your interests and needs are as important as my own.*

I promise to always share my thoughts and dreams with you.

I promise to grow with you so our marriage becomes a true partnership of shared dreams and realities.

I promise to always love you, through good times and bad, to keep our relationship alive and vibrant for ever more.

These are my promises to you.

The man could then use the same words but with some personal changes…

Him: *I Xxxxxx take you Xxxxxx to be my lifelong wife. Since the day we met, I have loved everything about you – your smile, your generosity of spirit and your zest for life…* then continue with the same promises.

The journey

I Xxxxxx take you Xxxxxx as my partner on our journey through life. I promise you that, as we set off on this path of marriage, I will always stay by your side. Family and friends may share our steps along the way but you are the one I want to be there till the end of the road. I promise to make the journey full of joy and to support you when the hills are steep. Let us travel together as long as we both live.

Fun/shared interest

Xxxxxx, Our love is like our passion for surfing. We started out hesitantly in the shallows before taking the plunge into deeper waters… with many wipe-outs on the way. Now we have the confidence to carve the surf together. Of course there'll be rough waters at times but our trust will support each other through the waves. Just like the ocean, our love will go on forever. This I promise to you.

Practice

Once you've decided on your vows, write them down, learn them off by heart and practice saying them, so you get the sound right.

Although you can read your vows, they will sound more sincere if you say them face to face. If you feel that your nerves will overcome you, there's no harm in taking a copy on a small card and giving it to Dad or the best man to look after. However, your guests won't laugh at any hesitations, they'll be delighted to hear your personal words and how much you mean to each other.

Reading

Many couples like to ask someone to read something special at their ceremony. Again, check that this is allowed and that there is time to do it.

Who do you ask?

The first consideration needs to be that your choice of reader is willing to do it, and has a clear voice so that everyone can hear your chosen piece. Most couples will choose a friend, but the groom's father or mother might appreciate being part of the ceremony. Make sure that whoever is taking part knows when they are due to get up and walk to the front.

What would you like them to read?

As always, you need to check that your chosen piece is acceptable at the venue but, apart from that, there is no limit to what you can choose except perhaps the length.

If it's a religious ceremony, there may be suitable verses from the bible. You may have a favorite poem, or you could use the lyrics of a song that means a lot to you both. A passage from a favorite book might also be a suitable choice. Some poems and readings give advice to the couple, others are love songs from one to the other. If nothing springs immediately to mind, there are lots of websites that give readings, but here are a few ideas.

A marriage... makes of two fractional lives
A whole: it gives to two purposeless lives
A work, and doubles the strength
Of each to perform it:
It gives to two questioning natures
A reason for living, and something to live for:
It will give you a new gladness to the sunshine,
A new fragrance to the flowers,
A new beauty to the earth,
And a new mystery to life.
(Mark Twain)

On Marriage

You were born together, and together you shall be forever more.
You shall be together when the white wings of death scatter your days.
Ay, you shall be together even in the silent memory of God.
But let there be spaces in your togetherness,
And let the winds of heaven dance between you.
Love one another, but make not a bond of love:
Let it rather be a moving sea between the shores of your souls.
Fill each other's cup but drink not from one cup.
Give one another of your bread but eat not from the same loaf.
Sing and dance together and be joyous, but let each one of you be alone,
Even as the strings of a lute are alone though they quiver with the same music.
Give your hearts, but not into each other's keeping.
For only the hand of Life can contain your hearts.
And stand together yet not too near together:
For the pillars of the temple stand apart,
And the oak tree and the cypress grow not in each other's shadow.
(Kahlil Gibran)

In marriage

In marriage, cherish each other in big ways
and in small ways, and never forget the
magic of those three little words
"I love you…"
In marriage, remember that it is the little things
That make the difference…
Don't forget the birthdays and the
Anniversaries.
An occasional note means a lot.
Share each other's life – even the small
Details – for too often we forget that day-
After-day becomes year-after-year,
And then it's gone.

Give each other room to grow…
We all need our time alone.
Keep strong your faith in each other; time
Has a funny way of testing us, and it's faith
That gets us through.
Respect one another… this world could
Always use more of that.
Speak your mind honestly, openly,
But with kindness.
(Anon)

Up-to-date

Modern poems or extracts from books, and song lyrics are covered by copyright laws so can't be printed out in full here, but some popular poems are:

Marriage is Love by Chris Ardis
I love you by Roy Croft
Love takes Time by Barb Upham
What does marriage mean in today's world? by Teresa Ling
Valentine by Wendy Cope

Music

You will almost certainly want a piece of music for the bride to enter and for when the couple to leave the ceremony.

The traditional pieces are The Bridal chorus by Wagner (Here comes the Bride) for the entrance and the Wedding March from Mendelssohn's Midsummer Night's Dream to leave by. However, many couples want different music.

Some ideas for the bride's entrance are:

The Prince of Denmark's March by Clarke
Trumpet Tune in D by Purcell
Eternal Source of Light Divine by Handel

Some more triumphal choices for the couple to leave to are:

Toccata from Symphony No 5 by Widor
Arrival of the Queen of Sheba by Handel
Te Deum Prelude by Charpentier

During the ceremony

If you want a special piece of music, perhaps while you are signing the register, again check that it is considered suitable. You may have a musically-gifted friend who would like to play at your wedding, or there are plenty of musicians who specialize in weddings. Surely nothing could be more romantic than "your song" played by a gifted harpist?

There are hundreds, if not thousands, of modern love songs, far too numerous to list here, and every couple has "their song". There are also many CD's on the market with selections of classical music for weddings. Some popular choices are:

Canon in D by Pachelbel
If You Love Me by Tallis
Clair de Lune by Debussy
Concerto de Aranjuez by Rodrigo
Moonlight Sonata by Beethoven
Ave Maria by Schubert

All these ideas will ensure that your wedding is unique to you – and only you.

Getting a Good Reception

66 A successful marriage requires falling in love many times, always with the same person. **99**

Mignon McLaughlin

Chapter 6
Getting a Good Reception

In Roman times, a marriage wasn't legal until the bride and groom had eaten bread together!

Perhaps you have dreamed of holding your reception at a specific venue ever since you were a child, but, if you haven't a clue where to go, it pays to do your research. Prices, food, standards of service and extras vary enormously.

The main venues for receptions are: hotels and country clubs, restaurants, pubs, social clubs, or your own home – indoors, in your garden (if you're guaranteed good weather) or in a marquee.

Variety of choice

Most hotels and country clubs offer wedding packages. These tend to include the meal, an evening function and, often, a night in the wedding suite. They usually have a choice of function rooms, depending on the number of guests, or might provide a marquee for summer weddings. Most will have a wedding coordinator to help you make your arrangements.

Restaurants might offer wedding packages, and can be ideal for the smaller wedding. Remember, though, that they might not give you sole use of the room and remain open for other clients. This can be a bit inhibiting if you decide to have speeches and toasts.

Pubs and social clubs vary in quality. Some will provide catering; others will provide a room but expect you to provide the catering (see later).

Home – this choice can be ideal if you are on a budget, and have a house big enough to hold all your guests (see later).

Marquee – this can be a very romantic choice if you have a large garden or decent field, but there are several things to take into account (see separate section later).

Look at your map

Keep distance in mind. If you're having a church wedding, you don't want to have to drive for over an hour to get to your reception. This might be especially important if your dream is to travel to your reception by a horse and carriage.

Ask how many guests can be accommodated overnight and if there is a special rate when booking for a wedding. If a venue is miles out in the countryside, some might want to stay rather than risk driving home late at night. If there is limited accommodation, see if there are any other places to stay nearby, preferably with a range of prices.

Careful Calculations

Always have a budget in mind when selecting your reception venue. If your budget is $4,000 and the venue of your dreams charges $100 a head, it means you can only have 40 people at your reception. If you want to have 100 people there, you will have to find somewhere that only charges $40 a head.

Don't forget to add in the number of the wedding party – it's amazing how many couples forget to count themselves when calculating costs. The main party might have at least eight people: bride, groom, four parents, best man, and chief bridesmaid, all of whom have to be included in the total costs.

If you need specialist caterers (e.g. Kosher) not already in your area, you will have to add the cost of transport for the catering staff.

How to work out your costs if booking a wedding package

Add together:

- Cost of meal x number of guests

- Cost of drinks package x number of guests

- Cost of evening buffet x number of guests (if applicable)

- Hire of room

- Hire of Toastmaster

- Hire of cake stand and knife

- Cost of flowers for tables

- Extras, such as chair covers

- Taxes (if not already included in prices)

Make sure there is someone to pick you up off the floor when you see the final total!

Hotels/Country Clubs etc.

Research

When you go to check out any venue, there are several things to look out for.

If there is a wedding coordinator, see if he/she makes you feel welcome on your initial visit. If not, he/she might have the same attitude on your wedding day.

If you are shown a very large function room, check if it can be divided in half, so that the venue can hold two receptions on the same day. This doesn't necessarily create a problem, but some room dividers are not soundproofed. You don't want the noise from another wedding to spoil your speeches.

Ask if there is likely to be more than one wedding at the venue on the day. Again, this needn't be a problem, and it often happens at large, popular venues. However, you need to make sure that both wedding parties are not arriving at the same time, especially if you want to use an imposing entrance or pretty garden for photos.

Food glorious food

Most venues will provide a variety of menus for you to choose from. These will usually be priced per head and will vary depending on the choice of food on offer. If you have your own ideas, most venues will be happy to discuss your requirements, and to give you a quote.

Again, many venues will quote for a drinks package on top of the food menu, usually consisting of a drink on arrival, wine with the meal, and a glass of bubbly for the toast. You are under no obligation to purchase this option; you might want guests to buy their own drinks, or you might just want to provide a drink for toasts.

If you want to provide your own wine or champagne, ask if this is possible and what the venue charges for corkage, i.e. a cost per bottle for using your own.

There might be an additional cost for coffee served after the meal.

Sit-down vs buffet?

Buffet meals tend to be cheaper than a sit-down meal. For a small, informal wedding, this might prove to be the ideal option. It might not be such a good choice for a bigger wedding, as your guests would have to queue for their meals.

What to eat?

This will obviously be a very personal choice. The easiest option is to have just one choice for everyone, although you should ensure that anyone with a special diet is catered for. Many venues, nowadays, will allow you to have two or three choices for each course. This makes it nicer for the guests but you will have the added responsibility of ensuring that everyone makes a choice by the required date, so that you can meet the venue's deadline.

The easiest way to do this is to send out a tick-list menu with your invitations. Hopefully, the guests will then be able to send it back with their reply. Make sure you send enough tick-lists for each member of the family and give a deadline for the replies. As your replies come back, keep a list of the chosen items, so that you can give it to the venue on the requested date.

A quick reminder

If you have asked guests to choose their menu beforehand, it is a good idea to produce small menus to put by each place setting. Guests don't always remember what they have chosen and this saves any awkward arguments with the serving staff. They can be run off on a computer very easily – 4 to a sheet.

Children

If you've got families with lots of children who are being invited, it might be worth considering a separate room for them at the reception. Children get bored easily and can be a nuisance during the speeches, etc. If the venue has space, the expense of a children's entertainer for an hour can be worth it, for the sake of an hour's peace.

Restaurants

If you decide to have your reception meal in a restaurant, ask if they are willing to let you have the whole room for the occasion. Some will be willing to do this for a lunchtime/early afternoon reception but may need you to be out of the venue so that they can prepare for the evening bookings. It is important you know this so your guests can be warned in advance that they will have to leave.

If the restaurant offers a wedding package, the tips are the same as for hotels and country clubs. However, some restaurants will expect you to do the organization yourself.

Menu

It is easier if you choose the main courses from the restaurant menu beforehand, rather than allowing people free choice (unless there are only about eight of you). This makes it easier for the restaurant staff to serve all the guests at the same time, and also allows you to keep control of the budget.

You can also choose the wine that you would like to be served in advance. Again, this prevents any large bills for costly champagne someone has ordered on the spur of the moment!

Pubs and social clubs

Most social clubs, and some British-style pubs, have a function room they hire out for special occasions. They vary in price, and some clubs will only allow a room to be booked by a member. Always have a look at the room before you book, as they vary in quality.

If using a function room, check that a bar is provided in the same room. You don't want your guests to wander into another area and stop there to drink, especially if it's a Saturday and there's sport on the TV in the bar!

Most social clubs will offer catering, or will know of an outside caterer. Again, it is worth checking their menu, as these, too, vary from excellent to poor. Word of mouth is a good test of the quality of the food.

If you want to do your own catering, check that this is acceptable – and see the section on catering at home. Some clubs will not allow this.

At home

If you are having a small wedding, or you have a very large house, a reception in your own home can be an attractive proposition. It will prove to be a lot cheaper and will also be a very personal occasion.

Delegate

Although you might well have done all the preparation yourselves, you will need to delegate on the day itself. Make sure you ask reliable people to help and that they know what they are expected to do. You want to enjoy the day, not worry about whether people have enough to eat. You don't want to be cutting up quiches, or pouring wine, in your wedding finery.

All the facilities

Your guests will need somewhere to leave coats, so make sure you've tidied one of the bedrooms! Work out if you have enough toilets for the number of guests. If you have more than one, it is a good idea to label them for Ladies and Gentlemen, making sure the Ladies' has a good mirror. A portaloo can be hired at a reasonable price if you have a suitable place to site it.

If you haven't got enough plates and glasses for everyone, you can hire matching sets from specialist hire shops, or many off-licenses (and some supermarkets) will do glass hire at a low cost. You can also buy pretty, disposable plates – a good idea to cut down on clearing up afterwards. Wedding serviettes and table decorations are available at specialist shops and many supermarkets.

Food

Call in the professionals

There are many small catering companies that specialize in providing buffet (or sit-down) meals for special occasions. The best way to find one is by word of mouth, but you can also look in Yellow Pages, etc. If you haven't tasted the finished result for yourself, don't be afraid to ask for some samples of the type of food provided. It is important you get what you want.

Always check what a caterer provides or needs. Most will bring serving trays, but you might need to provide tablecloths, etc.

Arrange what time the caterers are going to arrive at your venue. If you have to leave for your wedding before they are due to get there, arrange for someone to be available to let them in.

DIY

This is where a freezer comes into its own. Most supermarkets and freezer stores now sell ranges of party food, much of which can simply be defrosted, ready to serve on attractive plates.

If you have access to a cash and carry warehouse, you can buy catering packs of cold meat, cheese, etc. However, remember that some prices will be exclusive of taxes, which will be added at the checkout, so they might not be as cheap as they appear. Supermarkets will be happy to sell large amounts to you, especially if you order in advance. Some also sell trays of readymade sandwiches and nibbles.

Hot stuff!

If you want to serve a hot buffet, most of the ranges of party food from the freezer are ready to pop in the oven. However, timings are important if everything is to be on the table at the same time, and domestic ovens tend to be limited in the number of trays that can be put in at one time. If you are on good terms with your neighbors, ask if they would cook a few trays for you, so that your helpers can get everything out at the right time.

Alternatives!

If you're having an informal reception, especially if it's outdoors, try thinking of alternatives to the normal menu. Fish and chip shops and other take-aways will often deliver large quantities, or you could book a hog roast for a barbecue.

For real fun, why not book the local ice-cream company and get them to bring their van so that all your guests can have ice-creams for afters? They will all certainly remember the day!

Cheers!

The bill for drinks can add considerably to the cost of a reception. A local pub or inn may well be happy to provide a bar on the day. It will then be up to you if you want to pay for all the drinks or if you expect guests to pay for their own. If you are selling drinks, you will need a license to serve alcohol. The inn-keeper will usually apply for this. If you want to provide the drinks yourself, unlike a party, it's not really polite to ask all your guests to bring a bottle. Look out for BOGOF (Buy One Get One Free) offers at supermarkets or buy your bottles of wine a few at time when there are special deals on. They won't go off and you just need somewhere to store them where they won't get drunk in advance!

Champagne is expensive and you can get sparkling wines at a fraction of the cost. Many off-licenses/liquor stores will let you buy drink on a sale-or-return basis – and often hire out glasses as well.

Don't forget to have a good selection of non-alcoholic drinks on offer, especially if you have guests who are driving. Children might be happy with squash or juice, but try to get some more sophisticated ones for your adult non-drinkers.

Keeping cool

You'll probably need your fridge for the food, so you'll have to think of other ways of keeping the beer and wine cool. Many supermarkets sell bags of ice, so you could fill a clean bin with ice and pop all the cans and bottles into it.

If you go camping, or have friends who do, you might have an electric cool box – the type that plugs into a car cigarette lighter. These usually have mains adaptors and will keep drinks very cold.

Marquee

If you, or a good family friend, have a large garden or field, a hired marquee can be an attractive alternative to a hotel for your reception. However, there are several points to take into consideration.

Size and requirements

The first requirement, but one often overlooked, is that your area needs to be relatively flat! If you are using a field, you also want to check that no animals have been using it for some time before the wedding date. Animal poo is not ideal at a wedding!

The formula for working out the size of a marquee is to allow 20 sq.ft. (2 sq.m) per person. This will allow enough room for tables and chairs, bar area and a dance area. There also needs to be some space around the proposed area for the marquee company to work in whilst erecting it. Most companies will also provide a smaller tent for the catering, so space for this also needs to be calculated, as does room for the generators required for providing electricity. These generators will also need access to electricity from the nearest building.

The weather can be very uncertain so a covered passageway from the house is a good idea.

The outside of marquees are usually ivory and most reputable companies will be able to provide linings to complement your color scheme. There is also a range of floorings; matting is the cheapest, but you can also have wooden floors or, the most expensive, carpeting. The marquee company will probably also hire out your tables and chairs, etc. but these will add extra to the hire cost of the marquee itself. If you want to use slip covers and sashes to match your color scheme, they may need to be hired from a separate company.

Heating will usually also be arranged.

You will need to allow between 2½ and 3 days for the erection of a large marquee.

Spending a penny

Unless you have a large house with loads of toilets, facilities will have to be made available for guests. Most marquee hire companies will be able to provide (or recommend another company to provide) portaloos. These are no longer the blue huts found on building sites but luxury trailers with flushing toilets, wash basins and all the facilities found in a good hotel.

Parking

Unless you have a large drive, car parking can be a problem. There may be unlimited parking outside your property but, if not, let your guests know the best place to park.

Catering

See the suggestions for catering at home or in a hired hall.

Eat, Drink and Be Merry

66 Let us celebrate the occasion with wine and sweet words. **99**

Plautus

Chapter 7
Eat, Drink and Be Merry

The wedding cake originated from small cakes baked from flour and fruits to encourage fertility! Nowadays, it is considered lucky for the bride and groom to make the first cut in the cake together.

Once you've chosen your reception venue and the menu, it's time to think about the reception itself.

Getting organized

If you have a wedding coordinator, he/she should be there to greet you as you arrive at the venue. He/she will also tell everyone where they need to be – and when. If not, it will be the Best Man's job to organize your guests. This will start with arranging the Receiving Line.

Receiving line

Many couples think that a 'receiving line' is rather old-fashioned. However, it can be a very good idea, especially if you each have guests from various parts of the country who have never met each other's families. It gives time to put faces to names.

It need not be too formal, with a straight line, but the bride and groom plus both sets of parents can greet the guests as they arrive. They can be introduced to the other family with a brief handshake or kiss.

Tables

Your wedding coordinator will advise you as to the arrangement that suits the room best. The two most popular ways are to have either a horseshoe with a top table and two long wings, or a top table plus several round tables, each seating six to ten guests.

The horseshoe arrangement means that everyone can see the top table, however, round tables tend to be more informal so guests can chat to each other. It is not advisable to have a round top table, as the view of the bride and groom will be obscured.

The traditional seating plan for the top table (looking towards the table) is:

Chief B'maid: Groom's Father: Bride's Mother: Groom: Bride: Bride's Father: Groom's Mother: Best Man.

However, this can be quite flexible, especially where parents have been divorced and have new partners. Rather than stick to tradition and cause bad feelings, it is better to be more tactful and include new partners on the top table. Ushers and other bridesmaids can also be included, if you wish.

It is customary to seat closer relatives and friends nearer to the top table and others further away. It is also customary to alternate male and female guests, if possible. On round tables, partners can sit next to each other; on long tables it is usual to seat them opposite each other. It is wise to keep young children near their parents.

Speech time!

Making a speech seems to be the one thing that people are most afraid of. Unless the bride has decided to make a speech, her nerve-wracking part is over once the couple get to the reception. However, the groom and best man have the thought of it hanging over them for the whole time.

You might have booked a toastmaster, or your wedding coordinator might act as one at your chosen venue. They will announce the speeches after the main meal, when your guests should be nicely relaxed.

However, some couples choose to have the speeches before the meal so that the nerves are out of the way. If you want to do this, you need to let the venue know your plans, so that catering times can be arranged to suit you. You don't want the soup arriving in the middle of the best man's jokes.

You might want someone to say Grace before the meal. This could be the toastmaster or the best man. Graces are generally very short:

For what we are about to receive, may the Lord make us truly thankful.

We thank you Lord for happy hearts, for rain and sunny weather
We thank you for the food we eat and that we are together,
Amen.

Who says what?

There is a traditional order for the speeches.

The first should be made by either the bride's father, or whoever is taking his place for the day. His job is to make a toast to wish the bride and groom happiness and luck.

This speech can simply be that – a toast. However, he might wish to say something about the bride growing up, and welcoming the groom into the family. Another nice touch is to mention the happiness that he's had in his own marriage to the bride's mother.

Toasts

These can be very straightforward:

"Ladies and Gentlemen: I ask you to stand and toast x and y, the bride and groom."

The second speech is a response by the groom, thanking the father for his good wishes. He should then make a toast to the bridesmaids, to thank them for their help throughout the day, and for looking so beautiful. It is also a welcome touch to thank everyone who has helped in the preparation for the day.

It is usual to give small gifts to your attendants. If this has not already been done (e.g. you might have chosen an item of jewelry to be worn on the day), this is the time to present them. Some couples also like to give flowers to both mothers as a thank you for their help.

The third speech is the one that people look forward to most of all – the best man's speech. He should respond on behalf of the bridesmaids, and then make his speech. When telegrams used to be sent, he also read those. Although these are no longer around, it is usually appreciated if a few cards are read out, with messages from guests who are unable to attend.

If the bride wishes to make a speech, she should do it after the others have been made.

Calming the nerves

Everyone gets nervous at the thought of making a speech, but there are certain techniques to calm the nerves.

Whatever else you do, don't get drunk! One drink to steady the nerves is OK but, after that, anything could happen. You don't want to stray from that carefully prepared speech and start insulting the new in-laws!

Remember that the people in front of you are your family and friends. They are not there to judge your performance as an orator but to join in with wishing you both well.

Be prepared

Preparation is the key to a successful speech. Unless it is something you do every day, don't expect to be able to wing it on the day. There are plenty of books and websites with examples of speeches but try to make them as personal as possible.

It's not a good idea to write a speech out word for word, that will make it sound stilted. Work out what you are going to say, write key points down on cards, then practice on your own until you are confident. Fix the cards together in the right order, so that you don't end up getting confused.

Keep it simple

No-one is expecting an Oscar acceptance speech that rambles on for hours, remember the saying "short and sweet". Be sincere in what you say; this goes down far better than attempts at bad jokes.

Best man's speech

It is usual for the best man's speech to be humorous but this doesn't mean risqué jokes. If he's known the groom for many years, there are bound to be some funny stories from his youth that can be put in. However, stories about his exploits with other women are definitely not on the menu!

There are many books on sale with formatted speeches, and websites that offer to write the speech for you. These are great to get some hints and ideas, but the home-written one is always the most sincere.

On the tables

Always check with the venue as to what they provide on the table. Some will provide floral arrangements and use napkins to match your color scheme. Others will charge extra for flowers and you might want to provide your own.

The cake

The wedding cake is an important centerpiece of the reception. Traditionally, the cake was a three-tier fruit cake, iced with flowers and favors. Nowadays, there is far more choice in designs, from pretty floral through to zany ones showing the couple's interests.

Many people do not like the traditional fruit cake, so alternatives could be chocolate cake, or plain Madeira. You can also have different tiers in different types of cake. A fruit cake is heavy and will cut up into many pieces, so some people opt to have that for the bottom tier.

If you are going to save the top tier for a christening cake, fruit cake will store for the longest time.

Where to get your cake?

Although there are shops that design and sell cakes, you will also find that many cake makers are single-person businesses, with the owner baking and decorating in their own homes. They are often very skilled craftsmen and you will get an individually-designed cake.

Most will have a portfolio of photos of their finished items, but try to see a real one. Wedding fairs are good places to see finished cakes, and most makers will have a piece of cake for you to try before you order.

Some cakes need specially shaped stands so check if the maker hires or lends a cake stand with the cake.

Take time

Wedding cakes to your own design are not things that can be rushed out at the last minute. Although some professionals will keep readymade cakes in-store, they still take a time to decorate so order several months in advance of the day.

Bake it yourself

You might well have a family recipe that is traditionally used for family occasions. If you do, but don't have a family member or friend who is skilled at decoration, it is worth asking a professional if they would decorate a cake you provide. However, many will not do this as they have horror stories of being asked to make something beautiful from a cake which has sunk in the middle, or is burnt on the edges.

Another idea is to ask your local adult education center if they have a cake-decorating or sugarcraft class. You will often find someone who is very skilled and delighted to have another cake on which to show off their skills.

Ready made

Many supermarkets now sell plain iced cakes in a variety of sizes, so you can build up as many tiers as you want. You can then decorate them to your color scheme with small favors and fresh or silk flowers. There are many cake-top decorations to buy in any store that sells cake decorating tools and materials.

That sinking feeling

If you are building your own tiers, you will need a set of pillars for each tier. These are hollow and a good idea is to push a piece of wooden dowelling down through the cake and up through the pillar. This then takes the weight of the upper tier, otherwise the pillars might start to sink through the icing.

On show

Always check if the reception venue lends a cake stand and knife to cut the cake. Some will charge extra for the privilege! When you see the reception room, ask where the cake will be sited. Some will put it in the middle of the top table, but a small table to one side will often be more convenient and save it from being bumped or, even worse, knocked over.

Getting things back

After the photo of the cake being cut has been taken, it is usually whisked away to be cut into small pieces for the guests. Make sure that someone checks that the decorations are returned to you. In the excitement of the day, it might be the last thing you'd think of, but many brides have been upset to find that decorations have been thrown away by the kitchen staff.

This can also apply to your table decorations. If you want to keep the flowers, you will need to make sure someone is responsible for taking them home for you.

Frills and Favors

A trip round any wedding fair will show you that there is a vast array of extras you can add to your wedding reception.

Personal theme

One idea is to have your tables themed to match the interests of the bride and groom. Keen surfers might like to use a beach theme, with shells holding the name cards; sport fans might want to use their team colors.

You might also want to theme your wedding to the time of year. Christmas or Valentine weddings might be obvious, but Easter ones could have daffodils and Easter eggs on the tables. Autumn leaves also look beautiful for October weddings.

Favors

The original favors originated in Europe with five sugared almonds, symbolizing Health, Wealth, Fertility, Long life and Happiness – and what more could anyone wish for a newly-married couple?

If you want to stay with almonds or other sweets (love hearts, chocolates) there are many styles of container to choose from. Don't forget, though, that people often forget to pick them up and take them home. They could be costly litter left on your tables.

There are also children's boxes available to amuse your younger guests.

To save money, you can buy flat boxes to make up yourself and to decorate to match your color scheme, or cut circles of net and tie them up with a pretty ribbon. Make sure you have enough sweets to fill them. You don't get many sugared almonds in a 100g bag!

Other ideas

If you want to provide a small favor for your guests, but not sweets, there are many other suggestions.

Lottery scratch cards make a fun gift, especially if they are packed into pretty cards to match your scheme. They also give someone the chance to become rich at your wedding (they could then offer to pay the bills for you!).

How about a packet of flower seeds for each guest, with a message about "growing love"?

Some couples like to give separate male and female gifts. If you want to push the boat out, men might like an engraved miniature of spirits – these can be engraved with your initials or the date of the wedding.

Balloons

Almost any shape made in balloons can be provided by a specialist company, in almost any color to suit your scheme. Arches can look lovely at a civil ceremony or over a top table at a reception. Many couples like to have an arrangement of balloons floating above each table.

It can be tempting to think you can do your own balloons, but there are a few drawbacks. Most balloons sold in general shops tend to be smaller than those provided by specialist suppliers. This means that they have a shorter flying time so need to be blown up on the day of the wedding. Tanks of helium can be bought to do this, but you will have to delegate the job to a few reliable people.

If you are going to a specialist company, ask when the balloons will be blown up. They should guarantee to blow them up on the morning of the wedding so you don't end up with droopy latex!

Pearlized balloons look nicer than ordinary ones for weddings.

Danger!

Helium balloons are not flammable but warn your guests not to try the old trick of making the voice get higher by inhaling the gas. Helium can kill and is especially dangerous for anyone with asthma.

Evening Reception

The evening reception will almost certainly be a far more informal occasion than the earlier reception. It is usually an opportunity to invite guests that couldn't be accommodated at the wedding itself. Your invitations should specify the end time, so that guests know what time to arrange taxis, etc.

Most venues will be able to recommend a disco or other entertainment.

Peace and quiet

Weddings are usually times when people can catch up with family news. Discos can be very loud and many guests will appreciate somewhere quiet to sit in comfort and chat. See if you have the use of more than the main room at your venue.

Numbers

Check with your venue on how strict they are with numbers for catering. Some will be fairly relaxed and allow you to book a buffet for 100, even if a few extra turn up. Others are rather more strict and will have someone to count the number of guests on arrival. They will then charge you for the actual number and this could be an unpleasant surprise, especially if gate-crashers arrive!

The first dance

The bride and groom will be expected to dance the first dance of the evening. You might love dancing and have no worries about this, but you could also surprise your guests with a 'Strictly Come Dancing' demonstration. Many ballroom dance schools offer wedding dance classes, so you can amaze everyone with your twirls.

Chocolate heaven

Chocolate fountains can now be bought for you to set up yourself, but they tend to be rather small, really only intended for home and party use. For a large reception, it is better to hire a bigger model. This will ensure that the machine is set up and filled by the hire company. They will also provide the dips, sticks, and a supply of serviettes. Many will also provide a 'chocolate lifeguard' who will look after the machine all evening, making sure that children (and chocoholics) don't get carried away.

Wine on tap

A champagne fountain need not have sparkling wine, but looks better with some sort of bubbly. They generally take 16 liters of wine and you will need to provide your choice for this.

Make a bet!

Casinos can be hired to entertain your guests, usually Roulette and Blackjack. Croupiers will set them up for you and run the games. They are generally played with provided chips – you don't have to worry that your guests are going to lose their shirts!

Out with a bang!

If you really want to finish the evening off with a dramatic flourish, you can have a fireworks display. You can now buy fireworks throughout the year, but if you decide on a DIY display, make sure you have someone reliable in charge. Even just a few glasses of bubbly can affect the most sensible of people. In addition, you need to make sure there is an adequate area available and that you have permission from your venue.

This is one occasion when it is better, even though more costly, to rely on the professionals. Companies will set up and fire the display for you, so all you have to do is enjoy the sparkling display.

Enjoy yourselves!!!

Dancing Attendance

" Your wedding day is like a fairy tale; you've had to kiss a lot of frogs to find your prince. **"**

Anon

Chapter 8
Dancing Attendance

Bridesmaids were originally friends of the bride who dressed in equally fine gowns to confuse the evil spirits!

Who takes part?

Giving the bride away

Traditionally, this is the job of the bride's father but there may be circumstances where this is not possible. Another close male relative would usually be the next choice, but there is no reason why it has to be a man. Many brides choose to have their mother escort them down the aisle, especially if her father has died, or if mom has brought her up on her own. If you have children, you might like your son or daughter to escort you.

The escort should walk on the bride's left as they enter the venue.

Bridesmaids

Who to choose

Remember, the job of the bridesmaid is exactly that – the bride's maid. They are there to help you. Long gone are the days when the maid had to help bath the bride and dress her hair, but it really is useful to have a chief bridesmaid, one who will support you, calm your nerves, and fade into the background if necessary. Don't choose anyone who is more interested in pulling the best man or is hoping the photographer will pick her as his next model.

How many?

You might be from a big family and will offend loads of people by not asking them to be an attendant – especially if there are lots of little girls in the family who are all desperate to be a flower girl. There are always cases of "having to have cousin X, because cousin Y is being a pageboy". However, remember, it is still YOUR wedding and it is up to you. It's no good having nine attendants if you don't know half of them very well. If you only want one, then just have one. OK, so you'll have to explain it to all the disappointed families but better that than being worried all day because the attendants are arguing with each other.

Some civil venues limit the number of attendants you are permitted. Always check this before asking children to be bridesmaids, otherwise you might have some very disappointed little faces.

Chief bridesmaid/Maid of Honor

The chief bridesmaid will be very important to the smooth running of your wedding. She is there to provide support in any way possible, although telling you to change your mind possibly isn't the best way of doing it!

Before the wedding

If you live in a country where wedding showers are customary, it is the Maid of Honor's task to arrange it. She will often ask the other bridesmaids to help out with this.

On the day

She should be at the bride's house as early as possible, so that any last minute hitches can be ironed out with the minimum of fuss. She will probably go to the hairdresser with you and will certainly help you get dressed.

Other adult bridesmaids

These don't really have an allocated role to play except making sure your train doesn't get dirty on the way into the ceremony. They can concentrate on looking good. However, if you also have child bridesmaids, it is a good idea to delegate one of your older bridesmaids to be in charge of them. She can make sure that they all get into the right car, that they don't run off anywhere before entering the venue, and generally make sure they don't make a nuisance of themselves.

Flower girls and pageboys

If you're planning a wedding up to two years ahead, bear in mind that children grow up. The angelic little boy with blond curls you want as a page boy now might well be a gap-toothed demon in two years' time. And that sweet little girl could grow into a spoilt little madam who will stamp her foot at the slightest provocation.

Don't get carried away choosing their dresses straight away. A pretty bridesmaid's dress that suits a 10-year-old now will almost certainly not suit her in two years' time, when she might be a different shape altogether. Wait until you know the approximate sizes.

If you are having child attendants, always make sure they know what they are going to do. It is unlikely that they will be able to help you in any way, but they will look pretty!

Practice makes perfect

If it is your dream to have one or more flower girls scattering petals in front of you (check with the church first), get them to practice several times beforehand – using bits of paper if necessary. You don't want a heap of petals at the church door, and nothing left in their baskets as you go down the aisle.

If you want your pageboys to carry your train, first try them out with a bed sheet pinned to your waist. They can get used to the weight of it and also with walking in time with you. Some trains are fastened so that they can be removed for dancing later – you don't want to end up at the altar with 2 little boys and a train left half way down the aisle!

Best man

The best man's job is to support the groom, both in the wedding preparations and on The Day itself. Traditionally, it was usual for the groom to ask his brother to support him on the day, but this does not have to be the case. Of course, the job usually associated with the best man is making his speech at the reception and, whilst it might be tempting to ask someone who you know will be the life and soul of the party later, this is not always a good idea. You need someone who will take his job at the wedding seriously and will keep everything under control. You don't want to be worried on the day by little things that can be easily sorted out by a capable best man.

Although the name implies that the best man should be male, there is not a rule that says it has to be. Some grooms will choose to have a close female relative or friend to support them on the day.

What does he do?

His main job is to make sure that the groom arrives at the venue in plenty of time. The journey might include a swift drink at a local pub, but it is the best man's job to make sure that the groom doesn't linger there, or, even worse, arrive at the venue worse for wear.

His other very important job is to produce the ring(s) at the right moment in the ceremony. He needs to check that he has them with him before leaving for the venue. It is a good idea for him to keep them in a box or jewelry bag in his pocket, so that there's no chance of them slipping down through a hole in the lining, making him search his suit in front of all the guests.

He is also responsible for making sure that all the fees at the wedding venue are paid and for ensuring that everyone is able to get from the venue to the reception, if necessary.

The best man should be responsible for checking that all the hired suits, for the male members of the wedding party, have arrived in good order. He might need to collect them from the hire shop so make sure that he knows who is wearing what, and where they should go to – don't leave the bride's dad's suit at the groom's house!

Traditionally, the best man is responsible for ordering the bride's flowers and those for the mothers, etc. but, nowadays, most brides prefer to choose and order their own.

He might also, if there is no wedding coordinator or toastmaster, be the person who announces the speeches and cake-cutting.

Ushers/Groomsmen

The ushers' job is to provide help for the groom and best man. Usually, this is to show people to their seats, especially at a church wedding, and to make sure that everyone has transport to the reception afterwards. This means that they need to be reliable, turn up in plenty of time, and not sit in the pub until five minutes before the wedding.

Traditionally, the ushers are male but, like most things these days, there is no rule that says they must be and there is no reason why ladies cannot act as ushers.

The number of ushers will depend on the size of the wedding. Apart from in the UK, where it is usual to simply have two ushers, they should be of an equal number to the bridesmaids. Although, traditionally, the ushers were friends of the groom, nowadays it is helpful if at least one is from the bride's side of the family, so that he can recognize members of the family as they arrive.

After the wedding ceremony, the best man will escort the chief bridesmaid back down the aisle and the ushers will escort the rest of the bridesmaids.

Tokens of appreciation

It is usual for the couple to give a small gift to the attendants, to thank them for their help. If you choose to give the bridesmaids the traditional gift of jewelry, or cufflinks to the best man and ushers, it is a good idea to give them out at the rehearsal dinner or on the morning of the wedding so that they can wear them. Otherwise, they should be given at the time of the groom's speech when he thanks them. Other ideas for gifts are engraved glasses for adult helpers and soft toys for the children.

Other useful helpers

If you are providing buttonholes for the guests, you will need to have someone ready to give them out, and probably to pin them on!

Guests with mobility problems will be grateful if someone is there to help them, especially if the venue does not have good access (often the case in older churches).

Unless you live somewhere where sunshine is guaranteed, you can never rely on the weather to provide a dry day. It is a good idea to have one or two helpers with umbrellas, especially if there is a long walk from the cars to the venue. This could be done by the ushers, but sometimes they are busy inside the venue and not watching for arrivals outside.

Stag and Hen nights

Whatever you call them – Stag and Hen, Bachelor and Bachelorette, Hen Nights. Everywhere in the world has its own pre-wedding customs to celebrate the last days of singledom. Traditionally, it is the best man and chief bridesmaid's job to organize these events. These can be as simple as a night out at the local pub or as extravagant as a weekend away in an exotic location.

Whatever happens, they should never take place on the night before the wedding. After going to all the expense of a full wedding ceremony, both bride and groom want to be able to remember the day, not have to pass it in a hung-over state.

Of course, a Hen or Stag do needn't involve lots of drinking.

After all the stress's of preparing for a wedding, brides might well appreciate a day or two at a spa with a few of her best friends (and possibly mom). Or how about a weekend seeing the sights in New York? The more budget-conscious might like an evening in with a make-up party and a few bottles of bubbly.

There are plenty of action-packed activities to keep most men happy. A paint-balling day can be great fun (and reasonably cheap) or how about the chance to drive a racing car, or army tank?

In Canada, functions called Buck and Doe, Stag and Doe or Jack and Jill are becoming very popular. These are organized by the attendants and are for both the bride and groom to attend. They include music – live or DJ – dancing, drinks, games, raffles, etc. Guests are charged a small entry fee and all the money raised goes to the couple.

On the day

Whatever you do, choose your attendants carefully, so you can relax and leave all the tasks up to them.

Dressed to Impress

" After all, there is something about a wedding gown prettier than in any other gown in the world. **"**

Douglas William Jerrold

Chapter 9
Dressed to Impress

Something old, something new,
Something borrowed, something blue

Something old refers to old friends, and something new to your new life together. Something borrowed was traditionally a gift given to the bride by her family, for luck, but which had to be returned, and blue is supposed to be the color of fidelity.

The Bride

No need to rush!

Like all other clothes, fashions in wedding gowns change, so, if you're planning a wedding two years' ahead, don't be in too much of a hurry to buy your gown. Yes, it's exciting to go and try them on, but you can change your mind several times in the course of a year. You don't want to spend lots of money only to find something you prefer more several months later.

Where?

Where you choose might well depend on your budget. If buying new, the first choice of where to look will probably be a specialist bridal shop, either independently owned, or part of a franchised chain. Department stores might well have a bridal department within the store and many high street chain stores now have bridal ranges.

A specialist shop will have a range of dresses for you to look at, and often catalogs to order from. Many ask you to make an appointment before arriving. This is an excellent idea, as it means you will have the undivided attention of a specialist advisor throughout your visit. Changing rooms tend to be spacious, with mirrors so you can see the gown from all angles, and there should be plenty of room in the shop to walk around to see how the gown feels.

Chain stores will usually be the cheapest option, but the likelihood is that they will have a very limited number of styles. You will probably not have a specialist advisor, and you might not have the comfort of a large changing room.

You can also buy second hand, hire a dress, or have one made. Don't discount charity shops. Some charities have special bridal stores, where, as well as donated dresses, they receive new but end-of-line dresses from bridal companies. You could pick up a real designer gown at a bargain price.

Made to measure

There are designers who will make a gown to your personal requirements, designing a one-off, just for you. This will give you the dress of your dreams, but it comes at a price.

You might have a friend or relative who is handy with the needle and might offer to make your dress for you. This can save you money, but always look at something that she has made. Making a wedding gown is totally different to running up some curtains, especially if you have chosen a delicate fabric or a style that requires boning in the bodice.

Pre-owned

Your local paper or online auction sites will always have a selection of second hand dresses for sale, often at bargain prices. Some of these might never have been worn. Don't feel that they will be unlucky, or that their wedding has been called off – it might well be that the bride has put on (or lost) weight, or has changed her mind about style.

If you go to see a pre-owned dress, don't be afraid to ask to try it on. Check, too, to make sure it has been dry-cleaned.

When?

If buying from a specialist bridal store, some gowns can be bought straight from stock, but you will have far more choice of style, color, and price range if you have time to order. Most gowns from specialist bridal shops take five to six months to arrive.

You will need to allow time for fittings. There will usually be one when the gown arrives in the shop, to check everything is correct, another for alteration purposes and a final fitting when the dress is collected. The first two might well be done together, and there has to be time for the seamstress' to complete any alterations necessary.

Two's company

When you go to try on dresses, take someone with you who you trust to tell you the truth. Another opinion will be extremely useful. However, don't take too many people. They will all have different views and might confuse you or leave you feeling flustered from trying to please everyone.

You might think that you have to take all your bridesmaids at the same time, but this can also confuse things. Try to choose their dresses on a day when you don't need to choose your own as well.

Don't spoil things

When going to any shop to try on a wedding gown, avoid wearing any fake tan or other make-up that might rub off. You will not be popular if you leave stains on an expensive dress.

What style?

Be open minded when you go to look for your dream gown. You might have fallen in love with a gown in a bridal magazine, but just because it looks great on the model doesn't mean it will look great on you. Dresses in magazines might look beautiful but they have been laid out for the photograph, and pinned and tucked to form the perfect shape.

Take advice from the salesperson. They are experts after all, and they don't want you to look awful on your special day. Always view the gown from all angles – remember, your back will be to your guests throughout the wedding ceremony.

Make sure you have plenty of time to try on as many as you like. You will know your dress as soon as you try it on!

Tropical dreams

If you have decided to get married abroad, think carefully about your dress. Wedding gowns can be very heavy to wear and to carry in luggage, because of the various underskirts, beading, and boned bodices. You might want to choose a gown in a lightweight fabric that will be more comfortable to wear in a hot climate and won't cost you a luggage surcharge.

A reputable bridal retailer will be able to pack your dress, ready for you to take abroad with you. If this is not possible, you will need to fold it loosely with layers of acid-free tissue paper, and to make sure it is hung up as soon as possible when you reach your destination.

Tattoos

Tattoos are fashionable at the time of writing but will they be when you are 50? You might not want the leaping tiger on your bosom displayed to your grandchildren, so it makes sense to choose a gown that covers it. If you regret a tattoo on your arm, a flimsy stole or pashmina will hide it nicely without spoiling your photos (See also a tip in the Looking Good section.)

Underpinning

Dresses from specialist bridal shops will have usually been selected from couture ranges and, therefore, be made with built-in support, avoiding the need for a bra. Cheaper dresses might not have the built-in support.

If you need some sort of support, do get measured at a good lingerie shop. This is especially important when choosing a strapless dress. If necessary, take your dress so you can make sure there are no straps showing to spoil your look.

Veils

Try veils on with your gown before buying. Some gowns look better with a short veil, but some require a full length one. Always take advice on the best way to wear one and practice pinning it on before the big day.

Practice makes perfect

Practice walking in your dress, especially if you have a long train. You don't want to catch your heel in the train or trip over on your big day.

Goose-bumps

If you are planning a winter wedding but still want a glamorous, strapless dress, you don't want to appear with goose-pimples in your photos. So it's worth checking if a local gown shop will hire out a velvet cape. These come in a variety of colors and can look really dramatic – and will keep a bride warm in between photo shots.

Shoes

Choose shoes that are going to be comfortable all day – you will be on your feet for several hours. Tight shoes show on your face, and you don't want that to happen in your photos.

Wear the shoes around the house for a while. If there is any sign of rubbing, use a gel plaster – they're just about invisible and will prevent any painful blisters. You can also get party feet gel inserts to wear under your instep. These will make you feel as if you're walking on air.

If you're wearing shoes, not sandals, consider wearing tights or stockings – even if you normally go bare-legged or have perfect legs! They can hide imperfections, especially if the weather is cold and your skin turns purple.

Jewels

Of course, the most important items of jewelry will be the rings. Many jewelers offer discounts on wedding rings when you buy an engagement ring. Some will also offer discounts if you buy a man's and woman's ring at the same time.

Perfect match?

It is a romantic thing to do, but don't always think that you have to have matching rings. Not all rings suit all hands and you might need to try several on before you are both happy with the choice.

Allow time for the rings to be altered, if the store doesn't have your size in stock. You might also want to have the rings engraved with initials or the date. Again, allow time for this to be done.

On the day

Your choice of jewelry will depend on your dress. If you have gone for one with lots of embroidery and beading, it is better to keep your jewelry simple. A plain dress can take much more elaborate jewelry.

If you have a piece of wedding jewelry that has been worn in your family for generations, check if it needs mending or cleaning well in advance. Silver jewelry, especially, can tarnish if left but can be cleaned very easily.

Don't forget to move your engagement ring to your right hand, so you don't have to remove it to get your wedding ring on.

Bridesmaids

Who chooses?

It is YOUR wedding so choose the color scheme you want. Remember, the first rule of wedding planning – you will always offend someone. However, if you are asking your bridesmaids (or their parents in the case of children) to pay for their dresses, it is polite to discuss color and style with them first.

If you have set a budget for your bridesmaids' dresses, you will need to divide that amount by the number of attendants to see what you can afford.

Adults

This includes that awkward age between 11 and 16 as well as 'grown-ups'.

Don't be afraid to use a bit of imagination. You don't have to go to a bridal shop these days. Some high street stores sell bridal wear, including good ranges of bridesmaids' dresses, although the choice of color will almost certainly be limited.

Do you want outfits your bridesmaids can wear again? There must be loads of unworn satin numbers at the backs of wardrobes. So try shops that sell evening wear. Many have ranges of gowns that can be used as bridesmaids' dresses. There are also many shops that hire prom dresses, another good place to look – and hiring can save you money. Separates are also a good bet. Corset tops can be worn with jeans for clubbing afterwards!

Little girls grow up

Little bridesmaids grow very quickly and, unless they've got a party coming up, the chances are they will never wear their dresses again. So why pay the earth for them? Chain stores, and even some supermarkets, sell ranges of bridesmaids' dresses. They'll probably be cream or white but add a silk ribbon sash and stitch some small silk flowers over the skirt in your color scheme. Designer dresses – at a fraction of designer prices!

If you choose little girls' dresses from a specialist wedding shop, you will need to order them about four months ahead of the wedding. A good advisor will be able to gauge a child's growth and order a dress, making allowances for sudden inch gain.

Style?

Mini versions of the adult bridesmaids' dresses won't always suit a little girl. It's better to choose a color to match rather than a style.

Choose a style that is practical and comfortable for them to wear. As with the bride, non-slip shoes are a must! Head-dresses, too, should be light and comfortable so that they don't get taken off before the ceremony. Little children will almost certainly start to run around and play later in the day so be prepared for them to become untidy.

Let little girls practice walking in their dresses and new shoes.

Brrrrrrrrr...

Adrenalin can keep a bride warm, even on the coldest of days, but what about the bridesmaids? Even in the middle of summer, little ones can get very cold standing around while photos are being taken, so don't condemn them to being wrapped in anoraks someone fishes from a car. You can get woolen shrugs or cardigans especially for bridesmaids, and they will keep them warm while still looking pretty.

The men folk

Most men will say they don't like the fuss of dressing up but will almost certainly make the effort for The Day. It is usual, but not compulsory, to have the groom, best man, ushers, and fathers in the same style clothes.

For a small wedding, you can save money by asking the men to wear their own suits, possibly all having the same ties to match the general color scheme.

Tuxedos

In the USA and Canada, tuxedos are the usual choice for the men, though a dark suit can be worn for a less formal wedding. The usual colors are black or grey for winter weddings and white for summer. The groom will often wear a slightly different style to the rest of the men.

Morning dress

In the UK and Australia, morning suits with a waistcoat and cravat are the more usual choice for formal weddings. Again, these come in a range of colors, though black, grey or navy are the most popular.

Most tailors will offer a selection of suit styles and color schemes. Many couples will choose to have all the men in the same style suit, with waistcoats and cravats in the general color scheme. However, the groom can choose to have something slightly different, e.g. a velvet or brocade jacket, to make him stand out from the rest of the men. Waistcoats can be as flamboyant as the groom likes!

If you decide to have top-hats, check the size carefully. Appearing like a cartoon character with the hat balanced on the ears isn't a good look! And, if, it's too tight, it can leave an unsightly mark across a man's forehead. Your photographer will probably take a photo with the hats on – or being thrown into the air – otherwise it might be a good idea to simply carry them. Remember, they need to be removed before entering a building.

Hiring

It is rare for men to own a morning suit these days so hiring is the obvious solution. If using an independent local shop, you will need to book the suits fairly early on as they might not have enough stock for more than one wedding in a day. The shops owned by a chain will have more flexibility.

When the suits are delivered, always check to see that they are the right size, especially the shirt collar sizes, and that the waistcoats are all the same. It is not unheard-of for six suits to be delivered all with different waistcoat materials. If this happens, ring up straight away and request they be changed.

Kilts

Families with Scottish (or Cornish or Welsh) connections often opt for the men to wear the kilt. Again, these are available to hire and usually come as a full set, with a choice of jacket, sporran, etc. You can have great fun researching the family tartan!

Little boys

It is a fact of life that little boys would much prefer to be wearing jeans than a fancy suit. If velvet knee breeches are your dream, the chances are that only very young, or very well-bribed, boys will wear them willingly. However, there are plenty of options.

Tuxedos and morning dress for young boys can be hired to match the male adults. This will look cute but make sure that the children don't get too hot in them. Hot children usually mean miserable children – not what you want in your photos. Kilts, too, can be hired in very small sizes. Some hire shops will also stock miniature versions of military uniforms – ideal if you are having a military wedding – and boys will almost certainly enjoy the thought of dressing as a soldier or sailor.

A simple option is to have the youngsters wearing plain long trousers and a shirt, with a waistcoat to match your color scheme. This looks smart, is easy to wear, and the waistcoat can be taken off after the photos have been taken.

Taking back

If you are hiring clothes, make sure someone reliable is in charge of taking them back. You are likely to have gone on your honeymoon and don't want to get back to irate phone calls because the suits have not been returned. Always empty the pockets before the suits are returned to the store.

Mom!

It is a good idea for both mothers to check what each is wearing before the Big Day. While two guests can get away with wearing the same outfits, the same can't be said for the important mothers.

Some mothers decide to go for the same color as the bridesmaids, to keep in with the bride's color scheme. This can look very pretty but runs the risk of the bride's mother merging into the background in the photos.

Hats or no hats?

Hats are traditional for weddings but many women are nervous about wearing them. Some brides specify if they wish their guests to wear hats, but this can add to the expense for some people. It is usually best left to individuals to choose. However, it is usual for both mothers to do the same as each other, i.e. both wearing hats or neither.

Themed weddings

Themed weddings can be great fun, especially for people who enjoy dressing up. There are, though, a few pitfalls to consider.

It is important that everyone joins in the fun of a theme. Some people might dread the thought of dressing up and could spoil the day if they arrive in traditional wedding outfits.

You might dream of floating down the aisle in a medieval gown but will the men folk be as happy to wear tights? Unless you have a particular period in mind, try to choose something that everyone will be comfortable with.

If you have decided on a theme, let your guests know well in advance, so they have time to hire or make costumes.

Looking Good

" You were born together and together you shall be forever more… but let there be spaces in your togetherness, and let the winds of heaven dance between you. **"**

Kahlil Gibran

Chapter 10
Looking Good

Appointments

Book your hair or beauty appointments well in advance. On popular wedding days in the summer, the early appointments can be booked months in advance. If your wedding is before lunch, you will need to be at the salon early.

Don't forget that your bridesmaids and mothers will also need hair and beauty appointments. If you are all going to the same salon, ask if they take block bookings.

Order?

You should have your hair done before any make-up. If you put your make-up on first, it will almost certainly wash off when the hairdresser starts to do your hair.

If your hair and beauty appointments are at different salons, make the appointments to allow plenty of time to get from one to the other.

Some salons will allow a stylist or beautician to go to your home on the day of the wedding. This makes sense but will almost certainly cost you more, as you will have to make up for the time lost in the salon. You might also have to pay taxi fares.

Where?

You might be going back to your home town to get married so will need to find a local hairdresser or beautician. Do this well before the wedding. Ask around for personal recommendations if you haven't lived there for a while and have lost track of your old salons. You might end up having three hair dos in one day, but that won't matter if you get the right person in the end.

There are now many mobile hair stylists and beauticians offering hair and beauty appointments at your home, with special offers for weddings. These can be a really good idea but, again, always have a trial run first.

Practice makes perfect

If you are having your hair and/or make-up done by a professional, always have at least one practice run. This is especially vital if you're having long hair put up for the occasion.

Hair

Don't spoil things

Whatever happens, don't wear something that needs to be pulled over your head to remove to the hairdresser. Wear a buttoned shirt or little camisoles that won't destroy your hairdresser's work of art.

Arrange to be picked up outside the salon. It is very embarrassing to walk through town to a car park in your jeans… with a tiara and veil!

If you've got long hair and are having it put up, you might need to wash it the evening before. Fine hair can be very flyaway if freshly washed, and is impossible to style as you want it.

Hair ornaments on combs can slip out very easily. It is a better idea to use clips to fasten flowers, etc. into your hair.

Beauty

Don't try anything too extreme with your wedding make-up. Natural looks best.

If you are going to have your make-up done by a professional, always have at least one trial. Their idea of colors might not be yours, and you don't want to be stuck with something you don't like on The Day.

A trial should take about an hour and, once you are both satisfied with the result, the make-up on the day should take about 30 minutes.

Making it last, Kiss! Kiss!

Weddings always involve loads of kissing. To make your lipstick last, first use a natural concealer over your lips. Then apply two coats of lipstick, blotting the first with a tissue before putting the second on. Lastly, apply either a coat of gloss, or – a beautician's tip – translucent powder. Your lippie should last for ages!

Tears!

Weddings can also be tearful occasions and you don't want to look like a clown with black marks running down your face. Always choose waterproof mascara and test it first to make sure it doesn't run.

Moms will also find this tip useful – they are the ones who tend to cry the most!

Nails

Your hands will be on show all day, as guests will want to look at your new wedding ring. Natural color varnishes always look pretty but, these days, dramatic colors and decorated nail extensions are equally acceptable.

Whether you are doing your own manicure or are having it done professionally, allow plenty of time for those nails to dry. You don't want to have to take all the polish off and start again.

Don't forget your toes! You will be on your feet for several hours and a professional pedicure can help banish the aches. If you're wearing sandals, a pretty colored varnish – or even some nail art – will finish your look off.

Spots!

If a zit erupts the day before the wedding, try dabbing on some lavender oil or some toothpaste. This will dry the spot and take away the redness. If one appears on the actual day, don't panic. Use a concealer stick under your foundation and no-one will know it was even there.

Mind the strap marks!

If you have chosen a strapless dress, don't be tempted to go sunbathing just before your wedding. Red sunburn is not flattering, and white strap marks can completely spoil the look of your dress. An instant tan will disguise strap marks slightly but not fully.

A golden glow

If you are planning to have an instant spray tan, always have a trial session first to check the tone.

Have an instant tan about two days before the wedding. This will give the color time to develop properly. It should last about a week, so if you are planning an exotic honeymoon, you will still be able to arrive with a golden glow, ready to hit the beach.

To make the tan last, keep your skin moisturized. However, dips in the sea or the pool will make it fade quicker.

Don't mistake an instant tan for the real thing. It won't protect you against the sun's rays!

Winter white

If you're having a winter wedding but plan on wearing a strapless or low-backed gown, don't forget your back. It will be on show and you don't want the camera to catch the spots that tend to accumulate under winter sweaters.

An exfoliating back scrub will help, but, even better, treat yourself to a shoulder and back treatment at a beauty salon or spa. If you have lots of spots, a sunbed will help dry them up, but these are not recommended for constant use because of the dangers to skin.

Waxing

Have legs (and anywhere else) waxed at least two days before your wedding, in case you get those nasty red spots. This should give them time to fade but your skin will still be hair-free.

Tattoos

If you want to hide a tattoo, it might be worth consulting an expert. You can obtain specialist cover products that claim to cover them and other skin blemishes. If using them yourself, it is best to practice several times with these products as skin tone must be matched exactly and might take mixes of various shades.

Emergency supplies

A few necessities can be put into a little dolly bag to match your dress. Or you can get mom to keep them in her handbag. Lipstick will almost certainly be needed after all the kissing, and a hair brush, especially if you've traveled by an open car or horse and carriage. Your foundation should last all day, but you might want some powder to dab on if your nose gets shiny.

For him

It's not just the bride who wants to look good on the wedding day. The groom should have his hair cut a few days beforehand to avoid that 'just cut' look. It's probably not a good idea to try a new hair style specially for the wedding, so, if you fancy a change, have a practice run several weeks beforehand so it has time to grow out if you don't like it.

Designer stubble can look scruffy with a morning suit. Why not treat yourself to the full works at a traditional barber and have a proper shave?

The groom's hands will also be on show, especially if he is wearing a wedding ring. If you have a manual job, or love tinkering with car engines, try get rid of all the oil stains, etc. before the day.

Beating the butterflies

Last minute nerves

Hers

There's not a bride on earth who hasn't suffered from nerves on her wedding day. If you let them, they can spoil your day, but there are several easy ways to overcome your nerves.

Read the section on choosing your attendants. This is where it will pay dividends to have someone who is calm and doing her job.

Even if you don't usually eat breakfast, find time to have a snack some time during the preparations. Trips to the hairdresser and having make-up done all take time and it's easy to forget that you haven't eaten. You don't want to feel faint because of lack of food.

Space

Try not to have too many people at your house before the ceremony. Obviously, your close family will be there, plus your bridesmaids, but don't encourage the rest of your family to turn up for snacks and wine. You might love them all dearly but you can have too much fussing. If they insist, tell them you want your appearance to be a surprise – it usually works!

Allow a few minutes to yourself before leaving for the ceremony. Enjoy that last minute glass of wine or cigarette, if it helps to calm the nerves, but remember to spray some breath freshener afterwards.

Rescue

Take a bottle of Bach Rescue Remedy in the car with you. This is a herbal remedy that you can get from health shops and well-known chemist chains. A few drops on your tongue before you arrive at the church will work wonders.

His

The groom might well feel fine all morning – after all, it's not manly to admit to nerves. However, most grooms will suddenly get butterflies either just before leaving for the church, or just as they arrive.

Have a good breakfast (or lunch if the wedding is in the afternoon). You don't want to pass out in the middle of the ceremony.

Now is the time you will appreciate choosing a reliable best man. One calming drink is OK but more than that is likely to make things worse. So the best man shouldn't encourage you to drink more than one. If you have a drink or a cigarette, remember to use a quick spray of breath freshener.

Both of you

Superstition says that the groom shouldn't see the bride before the ceremony. But that doesn't apply to the phone. A quick call or text might be all that's needed to keep the nerves at bay.

Relax!

When you get to the entrance, stand still for a couple of moments and take some deep breaths. Remember what is important. You are going to marry the person you love. The rest of the people around are your friends and family come to help you celebrate, not to judge you.

Enjoy yourselves!

Arriving in Style

" Though it rains,
I won't get wet;
I'll use your love
for an umbrella. **"**

Japanese folk song

Chapter 11
Arriving in Style

Perhaps you ought to walk to church. That way you'll have more chance of seeing some of the lucky symbols associated with weddings. It is supposed to be lucky to see a rainbow, a black cat, or a sweep!

However, walking is normally impractical so…

Who goes in what?

It is the best man's duty to get the groom to the venue on time. These days, this usually involves booking a taxi (making sure it's booked in plenty of time) but, if the best man wants to do something original, he can hire a Ferrari, a fire engine, or even a helicopter.

Generally, the bridesmaids and bride's mother travel to the venue together, a few minutes before the bride and her escort.

What to choose

There is a vast range of vehicles and other ways of getting to the church on time, but you need to be a bit realistic and find out what's available in your area. If you want something different that has to come from another part of the country, you will have to pay a premium – not just for the mileage, but for the extra time that vehicle is away from home.

…goes together like a horse and carriage

Horse and carriage looks romantic but what if it rains? If you choose one, make sure it's got wet weather covers, otherwise that dress you've spent a fortune on will look like nothing but a dish rag.

Spare a thought for the horse

Before you book a horse and carriage, check the distance they will cover. Some companies will only allow their horses to pull a carriage for a couple of miles. If your dream is to drive off from the venue in a carriage, but the reception is a long way off, you might have to change to a car on the way. If you live in a hilly area, you might also find it difficult to book a carriage.

Cars

Something borrowed

You might be lucky enough to have a relative or friend with a super car, who offers the use of it on the day – possibly as a wedding present. This is great and will save you money, but it is worth checking if the owner has the proper insurance for the vehicle.

Also make sure you can rely on the owner to turn up on time with both the car and himself in immaculate condition – you don't want to have to visit the car wash on the way.

Take a look

There is a vast choice of cars around, and a huge variety in cost. Always go to see the cars before booking (or send a reliable person if you are trying to book your wedding at a distance). A vehicle that looks great in a photo or on a website might really be rusty or have bumps in places that show.

Make sure you know what the model of car looks like. Many brides have been disappointed to find a modern Rolls Royce arriving at her door, when she's been expecting a vintage one.

Don't be afraid to ask to see photos with the chauffeur in. You want someone who is going to turn up looking smart on the day. And don't be afraid to ask if you can see the cars at an actual wedding. This will give you a good idea of their turn-out and how helpful the chauffeurs are.

A good chauffeur will help you in and out of the car, making sure your dress or veil doesn't get caught. He will also take charge of your bouquet, so that it doesn't get crushed. He should also be proficient with an umbrella so that you don't get wet if it is raining.

The open road

There can be nothing more dramatic than driving off from your wedding in an open car, but make sure there is a watertight hood in case the weather is bad. They can be very draughty, so it would be a good idea to travel to the venue with the hood up so you don't get windswept before arriving for the ceremony.

How long?

When booking cars, always check how long they are available for. A church wedding usually takes around 40-45 minutes, with about the same for photos afterwards. A reputable company will normally say that you have got the cars for as long as the wedding takes (usually 3 hours to allow for travel time) but some will quote for the minimum time, e.g. 1½ hours, and charge extra for any time over that.

Some wedding ceremonies take longer than the average 45 minutes. As an example, a Nuptial Mass or a wedding with a musical concert can take up to twice as long. If you are planning a longer ceremony, always have the courtesy to discuss this with the car company.

If you want to go to a second venue for photos, always check if the company is willing to do that and if there is an extra charge. The cars might have been booked for a second wedding later than yours, and it can be very embarrassing if the chauffeur refuses to take you to the second venue because you haven't mentioned it and booked the extra time.

If your wedding is a civil one at a hotel, ask if the cars can wait till after the ceremony, so you can have photos taken with them.

How many cars?

You will need one vehicle for the bride to travel in to the venue, with her escort. If you have bridesmaids, they have to get there as well, so many couples book two cars. However, if you live near the venue, a company might be prepared to make two trips; the first with the bridesmaids and bride's mother, then returning for the bride. If you choose to do this, always make sure there is time to do the return journey, especially if your wedding is in a busy area of town.

Unless you are having a wedding and reception in the same place, remember that the bridesmaids have to get to the reception after the ceremony. Very little children might prefer to go with their parents and calm down after all the excitement and photos. If you have only used one car for the journey to the venue, it is unlikely that you can do the same after the ceremony. The bridesmaids would be left on their own, waiting for the car to come back.

Try for size

When you go to view a choice of cars, don't be afraid to ask if you can sit in one. You have to be sure that you can get in and out of the car gracefully, so imagine that you are wearing a full gown, not jeans. Make sure the door is big enough and that you don't have to clamber over a front seat (sometimes the case with vintage cars).

Don't forget Dad!

It is important that you choose cars that are big enough for your party. Your car company will be able to tell you how many people their cars are licensed to carry. If you have several bridesmaids, you may need a limo.

Decorations

It is traditional to have ribbons on a bridal car (or horse and carriage) and these will almost certainly be provided. If you want a color other than white or ivory, you will need to discuss this beforehand to check that it is possible.

You will find that most cars have some sort of floral decoration in the back. Don't expect fresh flowers as these are expensive and would add to the costs enormously.

Bubbly

If your fantasy is driving off toasting each other with a glass of bubbly, check with the car company. Some companies will provide this as a matter of course, but there are strict licensing laws in some places and they might not be allowed to provide this service. There should, however, be no objection to you providing your own bottle, but remember to ask someone to collect the glasses for you afterwards.

Weather or not…

Ask if umbrellas are carried in the cars. If not, you will have to make sure someone is on hand with one if it happens to rain.

Transport for your guests

Although most people have their own cars these days, many would prefer not to use them because of the drink/drive laws. It can make sense to hire a bus to transport your guests from the wedding venue to the reception (if the Royal Family can do it, why not everyone else?).

If guests are staying at hotels, it can be a good idea to hire the bus for the whole day and collect them. This can work out cheaper than booking taxis. If you do this, nominate one of the guests as the conductor, giving him a list of who to collect and where. You will need to stress to your guests the importance of catching the bus on time. Just a few minutes delay at each venue can make your guests very late for the ceremony.

Finding the way

If your guests do not know the area, put directions or the satnav position in with the wedding invitation. This is especially important if there are several churches with similar names.

Flash, Bang, Wallop

" Marriage is like a box of chocolates. You have to squeeze a few bottoms to make sure you like what you are getting. **"**

Anon

Chapter 12
Flash, Bang, Wallop

You will almost certainly find that your wedding day simply flies by. So you need to capture the day, either in photos or on video (or both), so you can look back at it and remember all the little details.

Remember that your day should be a 'Once Only' day and you won't be able to repeat the photographs.

Most of these tips apply to both photographers and videographers.

Who to choose

The old saying "You get what you pay for" is never truer than when it comes to choosing a photographer or videographer. Prices and quality vary enormously, so ask around for personal recommendations (or complaints).

Even if you've had a personal recommendation, always ask to see the photographer's portfolios or a finished DVD. If you've got time, try to see the photographer at work at a wedding. This will give you a good idea of his/her style and approach.

If you are having both still and video, it is a courtesy to inform each one. Most local companies will be used to working with each other, but it is worth checking to see if they are both happy. You might find that they contact each other before the wedding to check on locations, etc.

Insurance

There are several professional organizations your photographer might belong to. These are a good indication of the quality of his/her work but they do not offer any guarantees or insurance against shoddy work. Always ask if your photographer has got Public Liability and Public Indemnity Insurance. This should cover you against any mishaps caused by him/her on the day. But, also, don't forget your own vital wedding insurance, which should insure you against the failure of your precious photos or film.

Personal touch

The most important thing, when it comes to choosing a photographer, is that you are comfortable with him or her. Many people don't realize just how much the photographer takes over your day. From the time you arrive at the venue (and possibly even before that, at your house), the photographer will be there with you, recording every move you make. If you've booked someone you've taken a dislike to, it can completely spoil your special day.

Always ask to meet the person who will be taking your photographs. You might be very comfortable with the person who has taken your booking, but some photography companies employ several associates who only attend on the day and might have never seen you before. It can be quite a shock to find a complete stranger taking over your wedding!

Chains

You might be tempted by a special deal from a chain of photographers. These can often be very good offers but there are a couple of things to check.

The rep who comes to your house will have a variety of samples. He is unlikely to tell you that they are by different people. Most will be part-time photographers. This does not mean that they are bad at their job but they might be less skilled at organization. If the company is unwilling to show you samples of a specific person's work, it might well be worth reconsidering before you part with deposit.

Make sure the photographer will be from the local area. This might sound obvious, but some chains will send the nearest available photographer, one who might live some distance away. This means that he/she might not have been to the venue before, or will have had time to study it for the best settings. Also check that you know who the photographer is and that you have a personal contact number for him/her, so that if, by any horrible reason, he/she is not at the venue, you can make contact to see what is happening.

Friend or family

If you have an offer of photography by a friend who is a very good photographer, the same rules apply. Make sure he/she is familiar with the venue; if they live away from the area, ask them to make a special trip before the wedding, so you can be confident that they know where to get the best shots. Don't be afraid to turn down their offer if you feel that they haven't got the personality to control the guests.

How much?

There are huge differences in the way photographers price their services. This can make it difficult to compare prices. Don't be afraid to ask exactly what you are getting for your money. Some photographers will give a special deal for small civil weddings, or for mid-week occasions.

Check out:

Ask if the cost includes photos taken at the reception. Most photographers will include the ceremony and reception (up to the first dance) in the costs, but others will charge you by the hour. You should always make sure you know what's included before you book.

Check if the price includes photos taken at the bride's house before the wedding. If you want to have photos at the house, ask if the photographer has an assistant – or if he/she works with a partner. Most photographers like to be at the church to take photos of the guests arriving, especially of the groom and his best man, who should be at the church at least 30 minutes before the ceremony is due to start.

If there is only one person doing the whole lot of photos, it will be quite a rush to get from the bride's house to the church in time. Also, if you (the bride) live quite a distance away, it means you might have to be dressed in your finery at least an hour before you are due to leave for the church.

If there are two photographers, this makes life a lot easier.

How many?

The number of photos varies considerably. The ideal is for there to be unlimited shots. However, some photographers will limit you to a certain number, especially with their budget package; 36 might sound like a lot but these can be used up very quickly, and some less scrupulous photographers will then demand more money to take further photos. It is not easy to refuse on the day!

Always ask how many prints will be included in the final package and how much extra ones will cost. Again, this varies greatly and will, to a certain extent, depend on the number of photos taken. However, most packages will offer a set number, with the opportunity to buy more. Many photographers now offer a range of sizes, so you can make up a modern album with a variety of sizes on each page.

Giving away

Don't forget that extra photos can increase the final bill considerably so don't start promising everyone a copy. After the wedding, you can always show your guests the wedding photos and give them a price list so they can order their own, if they wish. Most photographers, these days, will upload the photos onto a website. This is usually password protected but you can give your guests the password so they can view all the photos and order copies.

Album?

Most photographers will offer a range of albums at an extra price, but, generally speaking, it is not compulsory to buy one from them. Many companies now produce digi-albums, where the photos are printed directly onto the page.

Formal or informal?

Most photographers will use the terms Formal and Informal to describe the style of photos.

Formal shots are those that are posed and organized by the photographer. You will be aware that the photos are being taken.

Informal shots are those where you haven't been asked to pose in any way. Images will be taken as they happen. Most people hate having their photos taken, so shots taken when you're not posing are often the best.

Another term you might hear is Reportage photography. This, again, is an informal approach, where your wedding will be captured in a photojournalist way – capturing everything as it happens. It is also sometimes called documentary wedding photography, where the photographer does not intrude or ask guests to pose.

It is vital that you discuss the style of photography you want. Most couples tend to shy away from the posed shots of yesteryear these days but go for a more informal approach, with just a few formal photos. If a photographer works with a partner, you will often find that one takes the formal shots, while the other is capturing different angles and perspectives.

A word of warning

If you decide to go for only informal shots, be prepared for a few moans. Gran will have paid out for a new outfit for the wedding and will expect to have a photo with you to show it off!

Schedule

Some couples decide to have formal, posed shots taken before the wedding ceremony. This is generally not the case in Britain, where it is considered unlucky for the couple to see each other. But if you have decided to do this, talk it over with your photographer, so he can arrange a schedule that gives plenty of time for the photos and for getting you to the altar on time. If you want other people in these shots, don't forget to tell them what time they're required, and where they have to be.

If you are having some posed shots, you need to decide on which ones before the actual day, and make sure that your photographer has the full details. There can be nothing worse than a photographer who continually asks you what shots you would like to do.

Most will have a general schedule to suggest to you, but there are always variations in family relationships and you want to keep embarrassing situations to a minimum. Your photos won't be very pleasant if Aunty Jane and Aunty Vera, who haven't spoken to each other for years, are asked to stand next to one another and smile.

Try and arrange to meet your photographer about two weeks before the day. That way, you can go over any last minute changes to your list. It is also helpful for the photographer to remind him/herself about what you look like. He might not have seen you for two years and your appearance might give him some ideas about suitable shots and poses.

On the day

The quicker the formal shots are done, the better they are likely to be. Most people get bored having to stand around waiting to be called, and no-one wants photos where all the guests are looking fed-up. This is where the schedule proves to be extremely useful.

Help

It's a good idea to ask a family member or friend to help the photographer with the schedule on the day. Even you might not recognize all the guests, so what hope does the photographer have? Instead of shouting to get people in some sort of order, the helper can tactfully get the right people into the right place at the right time! This is even more important if you are at a church with loud bells playing!

Trust the expert

If you have chosen your photographer because you love the work he's produced, trust him on the day. Don't assume that the best shots will be taken in bright sunlight. If he suggests a shady area, go with it. The final results will be a lot more flattering, with no squinting or facial shadows.

Second venue

Photographers will often suggest a second venue for photos. They usually have favorite places, such as parks or gardens, where they know that romantic photos can be taken. Also, you might have a favorite romantic spot where you would like to have some photos taken. Usually, only the bride and groom go, but some couples choose to take their attendants.

If the venue is the photographer's choice, he will check that he has permission to go there. However, if it is your own choice, you will need to make sure that it is OK to be there and that there is access for the wedding car.

If the photographer suggests a second venue, make sure it is included in the original price quote. It is not unheard of for the service to be added on later as an extra.

You have to take into consideration the fact that this will take longer, so you might need to tell your reception venue that you will be later than the rest of your guests. You will also need to inform the car company.

Moving image

A wedding video (usually a DVD these days) can be a lasting memory of your special day. Many people have their own video cameras these days and someone will almost certainly offer to do the filming for you. However, unless the friend or relative is an expert with professional editing equipment, the finished article is likely to be less than perfect.

How long?

The average wedding video will last around 90 minutes and, properly edited, will cover all aspects of your day.

You will need to discuss your requirements with the videographers, but, generally speaking, they will start filming about an hour before the wedding and go right up until the first dance at the evening reception.

How many cameras?

Although one person can film a whole wedding, two cameras will allow more flexibility. The same scene can be filmed from different angles, allowing more variety in the finished film. If they have two vehicles, it will also allow camera one to film the final moment of the church wedding and the couple driving away, while camera two is waiting for them to arrive at the reception.

Musical accompaniment

Most companies will use music as a background to the film. However, you need to be aware that you might not be able to choose your own. Music is copyrighted and can only be used if a license has been paid for.

Professional editing equipment will allow the sound of the bells (often very loud and overpowering on amateur videos) to be faded into the background.

Take a look

As with the photographer, it is helpful to see a videographer at work. Some might object to being inspected, but you can usually watch a wedding as a casual onlooker if you know where he is going to be working.

You don't want a camera in your face throughout the day, recording every word you say. The best films will be those where the couple and guests are hardly aware that they are being filmed.

If the videographer looks relaxed, then so will you!

Digital guests

Most guests will bring their cameras along, so a fun idea is to give them a blank disc and stamped-addressed envelope. After the wedding, they can download their photos or videos onto the disc and post it off to you. It's a great way of seeing your wedding from everyone else's view. It's amazing what you miss at your own wedding!

Smile!

Flower Power

66 I add my breath
to your breath
That our days may
be long in the earth
That the days of our
people may be long
That we may be
one person
That we may finish
our roads together. **99**

Keres Indian Song

Chapter 13
Flower Power

When you choose your bouquet, look at the meanings of the flowers.

Roses have always been a symbol of Love, but Orange Blossom has also traditionally been used for bouquets, as it symbolizes Purity and Loveliness. Carnations denote Devoted Love and Orchids mean Beauty. What more could any bride ask for on her wedding day?

Who's going to do your flowers?

Unless you have seen their finished work, be very careful if a friend or neighbor offers to do your flowers. Making a wedding bouquet is a specialized art. Just because someone can make a pretty flower arrangement, it does not follow that they can produce a bouquet that will survive the knocks of your wedding day without falling apart.

You will need to book your florist fairly early on in the proceedings. Many florists will only commit to doing a maximum of two weddings on a particular day, and the better ones get booked up very quickly.

You will need to meet with your florist about six to eight weeks before the wedding to finalize your requirements.

At the florist

Always ask if you can see a finished bouquet before booking a florist. Flowers that have been simply pushed into a foam holder will just as simply fall out. Many brides have arrived at the church in tears because their bouquets have fallen to pieces in the car. A bouquet can take some knocks, so check that the florist wires the flowers or fastens them securely.

Which to choose

Discuss your requirements carefully. Most flowers are now available throughout the year, the exception being spring flowers. A good florist will be able to advise you on your choice.

It's a good idea to cut out pictures from magazines when you see a bouquet you like. This is much easier than trying to describe the shape you want.

Take in swatches of material, or a ribbon, in your chosen color. Again, this makes it easier for the florist to choose flowers of the exact shade.

Ask if your florist has a sample bouquet you can hold. Informal, tied bunches are very popular but can be difficult to hold if you have small hands.

Carrying flowers isn't something that most people do every day. The temptation is to carry your bouquet at waist level. However, the flowers will then mask the upper part of your gown. It is better to drop your hands a little so the bouquet is at belly-button level. This will look far better in your photos.

Children

Check the size of the bridesmaids' bouquets carefully. Flowers can be very heavy, especially if they are wired. Little hands can find carrying a large bouquet very difficult, so ask for smaller ones, if possible.

Another option is to give your little attendants a small basket of flowers or a teddy bear to carry – these can be dressed to match your color scheme. Be careful, though, if you are tempted by the idea of a wand. Pretty – yes – but ideal for hitting other attendants over the head with!

Buttonholes

It is usual to provide a corsage for both mothers and buttonholes (boutonnieres in USA and Canada) for the main male participants, i.e. groom, best man, ushers and fathers. Some couples like to provide buttonholes for all the guests, but this is not obligatory and can add a lot of expense. It is a nice touch, though, to provide a pretty corsage for grandmothers.

You can have your own choice of flowers for the buttonholes but men usually prefer something fairly simple, although superstition says that it should be the same as one from the bride's bouquet. Large ivy leaves behind the flower can look like a bat flying across a jacket!

Although you might want everyone to have the same flowers, it would be diplomatic to ask the mothers what color they are wearing. Your choice might look awful on the mother-in-law's outfit.

The men wear their buttonholes on the left lapel and ladies on the right.

Most florists will provide pins to fasten the buttonholes. However, these can leave marks on fine fabrics and it can be awkward to attach the flowers at the right angle. You can get magnetic buttons – one attached to the flower, the other goes behind the fabric. These are ideal but might not work properly on thicker fabrics.

Romantic Valentine

It is so romantic to want red roses at a Valentine's Day wedding, but check that your florist is willing to do a bouquet for you – and how much she will charge. Florists can make big profits on single red roses on that day, and are also very busy. Some are unwilling to use their supply in a bouquet, or will charge a great deal extra.

Keeping fresh

Most reputable florists will deliver your flowers on the morning of the wedding. If your wedding is late afternoon, tell the florist. With luck, they will agree to deliver nearer the time so your flowers are kept in their cool storage for as long as possible.

If you have to keep your flowers at home for any length of time, put them in a cool place. Sometimes they come packaged in water; leave them in the packaging until you are ready to use them… but make sure there are no drops of water ready to spill onto your gown.

Beware!

Oriental Lilies have stamens that shed pollen, which stains. A florist will normally remove these before making a bouquet but if a friend is doing the flowers for you, make sure they know to do this. You don't want a bright yellow stain down the front of your gown!

Other flowers

You might also want your florist to make table decorations, or flowers for inside or outside your venue. These can include floral arches or small topiary trees decorated with ribbons to match your color scheme. If you want to take these off to the reception, make sure you get someone reliable to collect them after the ceremony – and that they've got a big enough car!

Throwing the bouquet

It might seem like fun to toss your bouquet into the crowd at the church but, once you've done that, you've lost it. Even if the catcher hands it back to you, it is liable to be damaged. Remember, there are likely to be other photos at the reception where you will need to carry your flowers. If you really want to carry out this tradition, but you want to keep your bouquet, you could order a little posy of flowers, especially for throwing. Another idea is to toss the bouquet as you leave the reception.

Preserving your bouquet

You can now have your bouquet preserved as a reminder of your special day. At one time, the only way to do this was by pressing the flowers (which can still be carried out). However, there are now firms that will dry the bouquet and mount it in a 3D box frame, so that it looks exactly the same.

If you choose to have this done, your bouquet will need to be kept cool. The firm should arrange to have it collected as soon after your reception as possible, while the flowers are still fresh.

If you decide, after the wedding, that you would like this done, many of the same firms will re-construct your bouquet from clear photos.

Happy
Ever After

“ Two souls but with a single thought. Two hearts that beat as one. ”

Friedrich Halm

Chapter 14
Happy Ever After

It was considered unlucky for the bride to trip on her way into her new home, so the groom should carry her over the threshold.

The honeymoon

No – definitely no tips on what to do on honeymoon! They can be found in another book! Just a few general points.

Where to go

Traditionally, it was the groom's job to book the honeymoon and surprise the bride with the destination. This sounds romantic and it certainly can be, but he should at least give the bride an idea about what sort of holiday it is likely to be. No bride wants to arrive with a suitcase full of bikinis and sun lotion to find that they are on a climbing holiday in the Scottish Highlands. This could mean the end of a very short marriage!

Passports

Check that both passports are in date. Remember, it can take several weeks to get new ones.

Ladies – some countries will not let you in if you have not amended your passport to your new name, even if you have your marriage certificate with you. You can apply for a changed passport up to three months ahead of the wedding, although you will not be able to use it until you are legally married.

Planning

If you are going to an exotic destination, check if you need vaccinations well in advance. You don't want to be suffering from the after-effects of nasty jabs on your wedding day. If you take your itinerary to your Doctor's practice or a Travel Clinic, they will advise you about needing anti-malarial tablets. If so, you must remember that, to be effective, the whole course needs to be taken.

In this unsettled world, it is also worth checking your government's website, in case there is advice on traveling to some of the more exotic locations.

Other websites will give unbiased comments on hotels and resorts. These are always worth looking at before booking, especially if it is to be a once-in-a-lifetime holiday, costing a lot of money. A honeymoon is not the time to be going for budget deals and second-rate hotels.

Don't leave it until the day of the wedding to get all your tickets, etc. together. Make a pack of everything you need, such as tickets, passports, insurance details, and put it somewhere safe where you will remember it!

Bag of tricks

Always leave your cases somewhere extremely secure, where your guests cannot get into them. In these days of heightened security, you don't want to be stopped at the airport for having handcuffs, etc. in your luggage. Similarly, confetti sprinkled throughout a case takes forever to get out of clothes.

Jetting off

If you're flying off the next day to somewhere exotic, allow plenty of time to get to your airport, and make sure you know the way. You don't want your first argument to be in a traffic jam when you're running late for your flight!

And a big thank you

You're home, the honeymoon's over, and it's back to work. The wedding seems like a distant memory but there's one more thing to think about. Saying "Thank you."

In these days of phone and email technology, letters might seem old-fashioned but they are still considered part of the etiquette of weddings.

Thank you letters don't have to be long and involved but they will certainly be appreciated. You might well have bought pre-printed thank you cards as part of your stationery package, but it is always polite to include a personal note and the name of the present, to show the sender that you've remembered what it was. (This is where the list from the section on presents comes in handy).

So, if you've got a pretty card saying *Thank you for your present*, you can just add in your own handwriting "John and I really loved the clock you gave us."

If you are writing your own letters, a typical thank you might be:

Dear Aunty xxxx,

Thank you so much for the tea-towels you sent us. I'm sure they will be put to good use when John does the washing-up! It is a pity you weren't able to travel to the wedding but I hope you like the photo I have included.

Thank you again.

Love from

Ann

If you've been given money towards a large item, a fun idea is to send a photo of the item with an arrow pointing to the "piece" the money bought. Similarly, if someone has contributed towards your honeymoon, a photo taken during your stay would almost certainly be appreciated.

Hi-tech DIY

With computer wizardry, it's relatively simple to produce your own cards, with a photo of the wedding. It makes a nice souvenir, especially for people who sent a present but didn't attend the wedding.

Let them have cake

If invited guests have been unable to attend the wedding, you can send a small piece of wedding cake with your thank you letter. You can buy special boxes to send it in. However, if you had a sponge cake, this might not be such a good idea as it will probably be stale by the time you get back from honeymoon.

Parents

If parents have contributed to the finance or organizational details of the wedding, it is a nice touch to send a card or letter to show your appreciation.

Good service

Many companies who provide services for weddings are relatively small and are often run as part-time businesses. Even though you have paid for their product, if you have received a good service, a little thank you note will be much appreciated. Personal recommendations make good advertising.

" There are three
things that last:
faith, hope and love,
and the greatest
of these is love. **"**

1 Corinthians 13, 13

Check Lists

ONCE YOU'VE NAMED THE DAY

Decide on the date
Ensure you have the right
   documents to book the wedding
Book a venue for the ceremony
Decide on the budget
Book a venue for the reception
Guest list
Choose attendants
Order stationery
Book transport
Choose color scheme
Book the date with the florist
Gift list
Make a checklist of dates for
   payments, etc.
Send out invitations
Keep a list of replies and numbers

CHURCH WEDDING

Discuss Order of Service with the
   minister
Book choir
Book bells
Choose hymns
Ask if photography is allowed
Check if confetti is allowed

CIVIL WEDDING

Produce correct identification
   documents
Decide a form of service
Choose readings, if required
Choose music, if required
Book the Registrar if getting married
   in an approved venue

HOTEL RECEPTION

Pay deposit
Choose menu
Choose drinks package
Book toastmaster, if required
Give guests menu choices, if
   necessary
Make small menus for tables as
   reminders
Table decorations and balloons, etc.
Order cake
Chair covers
Favors
Book rooms if people are staying
   overnight
Seating plan
Write out place cards
Final numbers for the venue
Pay balance

DIY RECEPTION

Order marquee, if required
Choose menu
Book caterer
Buy food if freezing
Decide who is doing what
Buy or order drinks
Crockery
Glasses
Order or buy cake
Table linen
Table decorations and balloons, etc.
Seating plan, if formal tables
Write out place cards

EVENING RECEPTION

Decide on the number of guests
Make guest list and send
   invitations
Choose menu
Book disco
Book other entertainment, if
   appropriate

CLOTHES

Choose a wedding dress
Book dates for fittings
Choose bridesmaids' dresses
Book men's outfits, if hiring
All men measured for suits

HAIR AND BEAUTY

Book hair appointment for yourself
   and bridesmaids
Book make-up appointment for
   yourself and bridesmaids
Book spray tan appointment

TRANSPORT

Decide how many cars are required
Book transport for guests ,if
   required
Inform car company if second
   venue is required for photos
Choose color ribbons
Send direction maps to guests, if
   necessary

PHOTOGRAPHY

Choose a photographer
Choose a videographer, if required
Discuss package(s) required
Discuss style of photography –
   formal/informal
Choose second venue, if required
Make a list of photos required

FLOWERS

Choose color scheme
Choose shape and style of
  bouquets
Choose flowers for bouquets
Order buttonholes and corsages
Order flowers for the church (with
  other couples if appropriate)
Order thank you bouquets for
  mothers

HONEYMOON

Decide where to go
Book holiday and pay deposit
Change name on wife's passport
Vaccinations, if necessary
Book transport to airport, if
  required

THANK YOUS

Make a present list as gifts arrive
Write thank you letters or cards
Send cake to guests unable to
  attend the wedding